SELLING HOUSES: EXPOSED

The Stripped Down Guide to Selling Your House Fast and for More Money

By

Brian T. Wolf

DEDICATION

This book is dedicated to my wife Christy and my children Aadra and Xander, who keep me striving to improve myself and my service to my clients.

A Free Gift for You!

As a thank you for reading my book I want to give you several additional bonuses worth $477!

Visit http://www.SellingHousesExposed.com/bonus
to download them all!

Contents

ACKNOWLEDGMENTS..7

'WEATHER' OR NOT TO SELL.....................................9

GONE IN 60 SECONDS (...BUT PROBABLY MORE).....................15

FOR WHAT IT'S WORTH...19

EVERYBODY'S WORKING FOR THE WEEKEND.........................25

ATTORNEYS, INSPECTORS, AND BROKERS...OH MY!.................29

ALL THE WORLD'S A STAGE.....................................33

DANGER, WILL ROBINSON! DANGER!..............................37

[WHERE] SHOULD I STAY OR [WHERE] SHOULD I GO? 43

COVER SHEETS ON YOUR TPS REPORTS?...........................47

REAL ESTATE ROSETTA STONE...................................53

    BROKERAGE TERMS 57

    VALUATION TERMS 59

    LISTING TERMS 61

    CONTRACT TERMS 62

    FINANCING TERMS 64

    CLOSING TERMS 67

SO LONG, AND THANKS FOR ALL THE FISH........................69

Appendix..83

A Free Gift for You!.......................................101

ABOUT THE AUTHOR...102

Brian T. Wolf

ACKNOWLEDGMENTS

This book would never have happened without the encouragement from my coach, Chaffee-Thanh Nguyen. I would also like to extend a special "Thank You" to Basel Tarabein, owner of RE/MAX at Home, for all his support and mentorship.

Get Your Bonuses at
http://www.SellingHousesExposed.com/bonus

Get Your Bonuses at
http://www.SellingHousesExposed.com/bonus

1

'WEATHER' OR NOT TO SELL

Let's say it clearly: No one knows where the market is going – experts or novices, soothsayers or astrologers. That's the simple truth.

~Fortune Magazine

I'll bet you're wondering when is the best time to sell.

Is it always spring?

A lot of sellers worry about missing the correct timing.

Should they sell in the spring?

Will they get full price in the fall or winter?

When is the best time?

In this chapter we're going to talk about the pros and cons of selling in the various seasons. We'll also talk about what you can do to maximize your pros and minimize your cons, so you can determine when the best time is for you.

It is a common misconception that spring is the best time to sell. Everyone seems to *know* that. It becomes a self-fulfilling prophecy where everybody thinks it's the best time so all the buyers and sellers come out looking. People are coming out of winter hibernation so there is a lot more activity.

Sellers have to look at what is best for them. If you are ready to sell, just because it isn't spring doesn't mean you shouldn't put your house on the market. There's no certainty that prices will go up between the current season and next spring.

One of the downsides of trying to sell when "everyone else is" is that there are more sellers, therefore there is more competition. You will have a harder time capturing the best buyers when they have more houses to see.

We find that buyers who are out in the winter and during the holidays are much more serious about buying. Clearly if they're willing to look within the confines of the holidays and brave the winter weather, they're going to be more serious. As I implied before, there will be fewer houses to see and so you can attract a good buyer in fewer showings.

A key factor to look at are the current market times in your area. Are things selling in 60 days, 90 days, or 180 days? Is your house a median house, or above or below? With that information, would you be willing to live with that kind of time on the market? Or would you be willing to price lower for a faster sale?

Let's talk about some of the strategies we will use to overcome the fall and winter "blahs" and get buyers excited about your home.

- You can bake bread or cookies. That fills the house with a warm and inviting scent. Smells are most closely linked to memories and a pleasant smell can trigger a welcome memory. Scented candles or air fresheners can work, but nothing beats the real thing.

- Keep your house a little warmer than you otherwise would. People are coming in from the cold, so make them instantly feel warm and cozy. They will then be much more likely to feel at home than if they were still shivering during their showing.

11

- Keep it bright - lots of lights! Every light that you have should be on for a showing and use bulbs that output the most amount of light for each fixture. This is not the time to be energy conscious. You're trying to keep that warm, inviting feel. Also, open all drapes and blinds during a daytime showing. Use natural light to your advantage!

- If you have a fireplace, especially a gas fireplace, you might consider having it on, assuming you'll be nearby to keep an eye on it. Again, it's warming, it's inviting, and it feels like home.

- The pictures I will use to market your house should be taken on a sunny day. If possible, plan ahead by getting those pictures taken in the summer so you have them. Maybe it's something you want to think about as you're reading this book and thinking about selling. Go ahead and snap some shots of your home so when you do go to sell you'll have them ready.

- Another thing to think about when you're selling in the winter is to keep your driveway and front walk clear of snow and ice at all times. If you are not able to do so you'll want to consider hiring a service that will get that done for you. You don't want to make it difficult for buyers to get to your front door. You want to make your home easy to get to with a welcoming entrance. Don't turn your potential buyers off before they even walk in the door!

- To prevent damage to your floors, keep a pack of shoe covers (I provide these for my clients) just inside your entrance. This way people who were trudging through the snow won't drag that snow and ice into your home.

The one thing I think about that's an advantage of looking at houses in the winter comes from my mother-in-law, who says, "If you like the house in the winter you'll LOVE it in the summer."

Brian T. Wolf

2

GONE IN 60 SECONDS
(...BUT PROBABLY MORE)

Time is the coin of your life. It is the only coin you have, and only you can determine how it will be spent. Be careful lest you let other people spend it for you.

~Carl Sandburg

One concern that sellers have is knowing how long the whole process is going to take. You don't want to get caught thinking, "Now I'm ready to move, let's get the house listed and sold."

15

Things don't usually move that quickly.

To start with we'll talk about some of the factors that can affect your closing. We'll estimate your closing date and some things you can do to make it work within your schedule.

First, let's estimate your closing date. To do that we have to take a look at the average time on the market for houses in your neighborhood. You should be able to find this from your broker.

But let's say the houses are selling after an average of 90 days on the market. Then we'll take an average escrow period of 45 days until closing and those are really the two numbers you'll need. 90+ 45=135 days, or just over four months.

If you want to move in June and it's now February, guess what?

You don't have a lot of time. You need to get started.

If you want to move in four months you need to list your house for sale today. Call me so we can determine the exact numbers and get you started.

Now that's an average time to sell, but there are times when things do move quickly...VERY quickly.

One Thursday a friend of the family called me to discuss selling her condo with me. We set an appointment for the next Monday.

As soon as I hung up the phone, I contacted several brokers that I knew worked in the same area to see if they were working with buyers who might be interested.

One did and we set up a showing for that buyer the next day. By Saturday we had a serious offer to buy and we hadn't even put it on the market yet. I'd call that negative market time!

A cash buyer can make the whole process move faster. Someone not needing to secure a loan and therefore eliminating the bank step will make the closing of your house super-fast, often in about 10 days!

Once you have a buyer, keep in mind there are some things that can affect the closing date:

- Is your buyer going to be getting a loan? (Most likely!)

- What type of loan are they going to get? Some loans can take longer to process than others, though many can be done in 30 days.

- Maybe the buyer needs to sell their current place. Have they put it on the market? Do they have a contract?

These are things you'll need to know before you can solidify a closing date. Keep in mind the closing date can be negotiated like other terms of the contract.

If the closing date is most important to you, be willing to give in on other terms such as price, mortgage contingency, or other contingencies. Also keep in mind short sales can take significantly longer.

* To get some more information on short sales, check out http://www.SellingHousesExposed.com/bonus for a detailed explanation of the short sale process.

3

FOR WHAT IT'S WORTH

The most influential factor in selling a home is always price. Don't build 'wiggle room' into the asking price. There's a price war out there and you have to win it from the get-go.

~Barbara Corcoran

There are three main factors that determine whether a house will sell:

- Location
- Condition
- Price

I don't think you're planning on putting your house on wheels and shipping it to another piece of land, so there's nothing we can do about the first one. We'll discuss condition in "To Stage or Not to Stage" (Chapter 6.) For now let's focus on setting the right price.

How do we figure out a home's value?

The short answer is when we are determining what your house is worth we look at the comps. What is a comp? A comp is short for "comparable sale." So we want to find a sale in your neighborhood of a comparable home and use that, preferably more than one, to determine what your house should sell for.

When you're going through the Internet looking for data you're going to run across many sites that give you an estimated value of your home. This is not to be used as a comp.

Why? These free sites are not actually offering to buy your house; it's not necessarily a realistic determination of value. However, it can get you in the ballpark. They're not usually off by 100%. In other words, if they say your home is worth $200,000 there's an extremely likely chance that it's NOT going to sell for $500,000.

*Check out "Why FREE Real Estate Sites are Worth the   Cost"   at
http://www.SellingHousesExposed.com/bonus

When we are looking for comps we're not likely to find an identical house in identical condition in your exact neighborhood - so we will have to make some adjustments to the houses we do find.

In addition, banks are usually going to look at a one mile radius around your house within the last 12 months. (Only 6 if the market is rapidly declining, as we saw in 2008 and 2009.)

Now you may wonder why the bank's opinion matters. Well the bank's opinion is going to come from an appraisal. And that appraisal can be very important to a buyer needing a loan to buy your house. If they can't get the right appraisal they can't get the loan and they can't buy your house.

So what do WE look for when we're determining comps?

First I'm going to run a search within a one-mile radius – or, if the houses are much more densely located, a smaller geographical area – of sales in the last 6-12 months and we're going to compare some types.

21

We're going to look at a ranch, a 2 story, and a split level. We are going to look at the lot size. What is the land worth in your neighborhood? When we're looking at these houses that have come up we're going to look at both the closed sales and the pending sales and what's currently on the market.

In addition to pricing we're going to see what our market time should be and what your competition is. So we will get a median price value of your neighborhood AND a median market time.

* For anyone who skipped statistics class, the median is the number in a range where half of the points are larger and half are smaller. Go to http://www.SellingHousesExposed.com/bonus for some examples of finding median house values.

Getting back to our analysis, say for instance the median price in your neighborhood is $300,000 and the median market time is 60 days, then all other things being equal, if you price at $300,000 you can expect to sell in 60 days.

If you're willing to wait a little longer you might price a little higher. If you need to sell sooner you might consider selling a little lower.

So what are the other things that we look at to determine value?

Price per square foot can be very useful in determining value. Even if the houses in your area are not like yours, you can take the average price per square foot of those houses and get a ballpark estimate for yours.

We can also look at the improvements or the features that are or are not in your home. We can then add or subtract from the value accordingly.

(http://www.SellingHousesExposed.com/bonus has a sample CMA you can view.)

We'll also look at what your buyer's best alternative is to buying your house. Clearly, if a more updated house with a bigger lot or more square footage is for sale at a lower price in your neighborhood, you're overpriced.

We may find the opposite: a more comparable house on the market for a higher dollar amount. But keep in mind, if it's been on the market a long time they are likely overpriced as well.

We have to get the right price in the beginning to ultimately get the higher price. If we don't price it correctly to begin with we'll have to make a series of price reductions. Price reductions show desperation and can lead to an even lower price than we would have gotten had we priced it correctly to begin with.

It will be evident though, even if we think we priced it correctly but the market tells us otherwise (the evidence being we won't be getting any showings or offers) then we will obviously consider reducing the price as needed.

* If you want to see what the value of various improvements can do to your home, go to http://www.SellingHousesExposed.com/bonus for a guide on the projected return on investment of various home improvement projects.

4

EVERYBODY'S WORKING FOR THE WEEKEND

I agree with Balzac and 19th-century writers, black and white, who say, "I write for money." Yes, I think everybody should be paid handsomely; I insist on it, and I pay people who work for me, or with me, handsomely.

~Maya Angelou

The question everyone wants to dance around is how much you should pay your broker to sell your house. I'm not sure why people get so squeamish about pricing.

25

It's common in sales to postpone that discussion.

However, let's get right into this and I'm going to directly answer the question.

Again the question is how much should a seller pay a broker to sell their house?

The answer is: you don't!

The buyer does.

I mean, seriously, who brings the money to the closing?

The seller?

Not usually.

It's almost always the buyer who is bringing money to closing.

That money gets divided many different ways; the bulk of it (hopefully) going to you, the seller.

Now with that being said, it is up to the seller to agree on what percentage the broker ultimately receives, so this is a valid discussion. Before we get into that let's talk about how much you pay other professionals.

Keep in mind that you have a professional by your side who is legally bound to be your fiduciary and your advocate.

Think about how much you tip at a restaurant.

Our society says the standard is 15%, though most of us who've worked in that industry in the past tip more than that. A talent agent makes at least 10%. Commission-based sales reps can earn at least 15%. Many insurance agents start at 25%.

Are you starting to get an idea of what ballpark we should be in?

Keep in mind the broker handling your sale isn't the only one that is getting paid.

Brokers have to share with their office and with the buyer's broker so the percentage you are paying is getting split many different ways.

It also needs to cover all the marketing that was done to sell the house.

To see all the ways a brokerage commission can be split up, visit http://www.SellingHousesExposed.com/bonus for a handy chart.

Your agent takes on significant expenses up front to market your house and so they're motivated to get you what you want in the time frame you want.

And they are only paid if they are successful.

According to the National Association of REALTORS™ (NAR) the average house sold by a broker sells for 18% more than those sold by owner.

Clearly you can see that when most brokers charge 6% you are getting a bargain. I have seen sellers willing to pay 7-10% to have a committed and motivated agent handle their sale – and even still they come out ahead.

No one wants to throw money away or pay more than they have to. That's why I wrote this book to show you everything you need to expect your broker to do to earn their commission.

It's important to do your homework upfront and make the right choice so you can save money.

5

ATTORNEYS, INSPECTORS, AND BROKERS...OH MY!

ASSEMBLE THE BEST TEAM FOR YOUR CLOSING

Individual commitment to a group effort – that is what makes a team work, a company work, a society work, a civilization work.
~Vince Lombardi

It takes several experienced professionals working together to make your sale as smooth and profitable as it can be!

29

As we discussed in the chapter "Everybody's Working for the Weekend" your real estate professional is the most valuable person on your team (aside from you of course!). Once you've hired him it's time to assemble the rest.

Even if you have a solid relationship with a service provider, it's a good idea to find out who your broker works with most often. After all, you want this to go well and your broker's team should already be used to working together.

The first person on your team is the home inspector. You're probably thinking:

"Isn't the home inspection the buyer's responsibility?!"

Certainly I recommend every buyer get a professional home inspection, but as a seller it can be a good idea to find out ahead of time all of the things an inspector might find. If you've been in the house awhile you could be surprised by what comes up.

*To see a sample inspection report, visit http://www.SellingHousesExposed.com/bonus

The next hire is going to be your attorney. Once we have an accepted purchase contract from a qualified buyer, you are going to need your attorney to review the contract, prepare the deed, and review the title (among other things!).

The attorney will also help with hiring the title company. Having a good working relationship makes this part mostly invisible to both the seller and the buyer. A few of the top companies are national which can you help tremendously if you are selling out of state.

Each member of your team adds a layer of protection for you and confidence that you will receive the best possible closing experience. It's never too soon to get in touch with your providers and start the planning process.

I have a team of extremely qualified professionals that I provide to all of my clients. You won't have to hunt around looking for your team. I make this whole process easy for you because I have everything you need ready to start on day one.

6

ALL THE WORLD'S A STAGE

**If you want to sell your car, what do you do?
You clean and polish it and make it the best
you can.**

~Paul Arden

There are a lot of opinions about whether you should stage your house for sale or not. So we ask, to stage or not to stage?

Frankly that question really needs to be answered by first defining the word *staging*. Are we talking about self-staging or Realtor™-assisted staging or are we talking about professional staging? So let's talk about:

33

- What we mean by staging

- When should we stage?

- And how to do it.

When most people are talking about whether to stage they are talking about professional staging (this can even include furniture rental.) This can be actually more reasonable than you expect. And you'll need to consult with your broker to determine whether it's really necessary for your property. Though for the low cost you can get a much higher valuation, so really it comes down to what your budget is and can you afford the upfront cost.

If you have a move-in ready property that's vacant, staging is a MUST. You need to have that furniture to showcase the size. My advice is if you can get professional staging for a cost that's less than one month of carrying the property empty, it's well worth it.

So let's focus mostly on Realtor™-assisted staging or self-staging. And using that definition you should ALWAYS, ALWAYS, ALWAYS stage your home.

We want a buyer to feel comfortable. We want your home to feel updated and move-in ready. We want everyone walking in your door to feel like they have to live there NOW. By creating a welcoming environment, we will get you the most money for your property.

34

One thing that is a MUST – It must be clean.

I know this can be a pain especially when you're living in your house while you're trying to sell it. If you have to leave for work, you have to make sure your house is clean because somebody might want to come see it.

So that means a daily routine.

Make sure everyone in your household is on board with a cleaning routine. Tidy up daily. Put away dishes. Pick up shoes. If you keep up with this on a daily basis, it will easily become your routine and will help keep your home in showing shape.

One of the best ways to help keep your house tidy is by boxing away anything you can do without for the next 4 to 6 months. And this will even help you get a head start on your packing!

As far as furniture goes keep it spare. One or two pieces of furniture to a room are really all that is needed to give the dimensions and make a buyer understand how large the space is. Any more than that and it'll look crowded. Any less and it's going to feel small.

This surprised me when I got into business. I was used to seeing homes that were empty, and personally I like to look at them that way. But the average buyer does not.

Keep in mind your competition is not doing this.

Except for the homes that sell quickly. They are.

If you want yours to be one of the homes that sells quickly you've got to take these steps.

When you are organizing and staging keep your buyer in mind. They are looking for their next house, not yours. Collectibles and quirky kitsch can be distracting. Get them out of there. A buyer can spend 20 minutes looking at your collection of autographed baseballs and not realize they aren't paying attention to the house. They might only remember your baseball collection and not all the wonderful features of your home. Put it out of sight.

As I mentioned, if you can live without it for 4 to 6 months, box it up.

For pictures of more staging ideas visit http://www.SellingHousesExposed.com/bonus.

7

DANGER, WILL ROBINSON! DANGER!

I have six locks on my door all in a row. When I go out, I lock every other one. I figure no matter how long somebody stands there picking the locks, they are always locking three.

~Elayne Boosler

As a Realtor™, I get asked a number of questions about security.

What are the security risks about showing?

Who's going to be in my house?

Is it secure?

Sellers have a very valid right to be concerned about the safety of their pets, potential for missing valuables, safety of their children and their family, and potential property damage when strangers are coming through hoping to buy their house.

It's absolutely valid and it's ok to be concerned.

In fact, we should all pay better attention to security in general.

One time I was showing coach homes in Vernon Hills. I needed to find Unit B, but the units weren't labeled. I went inside the building, but couldn't find anything labeled Unit B. I knew it was an upstairs unit and since there were only two units I knew I had a 50/50 shot at picking the right door. I chose the door on the left and knocked. There was no answer, so I turned the key and opened the door. My clients and I went inside and started to look around.

One of the bedroom doors was closed so I knocked just to see if anyone was there before I went in. I heard noises from behind the door. When I opened it, a sleepy gentleman looked up and demanded to know who we were.

I told him I was with RE/MAX and we were showing the house for sale.

He said his house wasn't for sale and that we needed to get out of there. I told him my key opened the door!

He said, "Well, I don't lock my door."

What?! You don't lock your door? I wanted to scream.

"I'm very sorry!" was all I could offer.

So we left, went across the hall and, sure enough, that was the correct unit.

This story illustrates that at a **minimum** you must keep your doors locked. Even in a condo situation where there's a secure entrance outside, you want to make sure that anyone that gets inside the building can't just walk into your home.

Here are some more things I recommend to my clients in order to make them feel more secure, especially when we are planning on showing their home to potential buyers.

Do not let anyone into your house who does not have a prearranged appointment. My office will schedule all showing appointments and let you know who to expect and when to expect them.

- Anyone that does show up at your door unexpectedly, whether they are a buyer or an agent, should be directed to your agent's office.

- If there's not a sign out front of your home make sure you have a few of your agent's business cards available. You can hand them out when someone knocks on your door to inquire about the property. This is to protect you as much as anything.

- We will place a lock box with your permission on your home that only agents will have access to. This again makes sure random strangers are not walking through your house.

- If you have pets, we need to develop a plan for them. Will they be locked up during the day and/or during showings? Are they friendly with strangers? Perhaps you can take your dog for a walk during showings. There are options and we will figure out the best one for you.

These are all questions we'll need to address and develop in our plan.

Let's also develop a plan for your valuables. Make sure they are all put away. Keep an inventory of your valuables. And after every showing verify they are all there. That way if something does turn up missing we will know who was through more recently and have a better chance of figuring out what happened.

You should always, ALWAYS plan to be outside or away from home during each showing.

Feel free to go out to dinner, catch a movie, or go for a walk. Sometimes you might even sit in your car. It's ok to wait at home until the agent shows up, but it's best to be prepared to go ahead and go out when they arrive. A buyer feels more comfortable and much more at home when the owner is not there, even if you're in another room. A current homeowner can make potential buyers feel nervous and uncomfortable—which is the opposite of how we want to make them feel! We want a buyer to feel at home. We want them to feel like it is their home. They'll be more likely to make a good offer.

Another thing we do is keep shoe covers near your front door. We can require that anyone coming through your home take their shoes off. This will help keep your carpets clean. If that's not a good option, we could use runners on the carpet that will help actually create a tour and help guide people through your house.

Another thing to do at the beginning of the whole process is to take pictures of your property along with your home inventory.

41

This will help document your property along with all your stuff in case of a loss or damage. We also want to make sure we don't give out your garage door code, if you have one, unless there are certain exceptions that we'll get into later.

When you work with me we'll go over these preventative measures and more to ensure the safety of your pets and house.

* Contact me and we'll formulate a specific plan of action for you. In the meantime, download the free security checklist from
http://www.SellingHousesExposed.com/bonus

8

[WHERE] SHOULD I STAY OR [WHERE] SHOULD I GO?

Your present circumstances don't determine where you can go; they merely determine where you start.

~Nido Qubein

When you're about to sell the house you're living in there is a moment when you're going to be thinking...

Oh my gosh, where am I going to live?

The question inevitably comes up: do you sell first and then look for something to buy or do you buy first and then sell?

It really is going to vary from market to market, however even in a sellers' market you're likely going to want to sell first.

The first question you'll need to answer is whether you have to sell in order to buy. If you can afford to buy your next place before selling the one you're in then you have more options.

For our purposes today let's assume that you need to sell your house before you can buy a new one.

In almost every case you're going to need to at least list your house for sale before you start looking for one to purchase. The obvious dilemma you're going to run into is what if you sell first and you're not able to find a house to buy, what do you do?

One common option is to rent your house back from the new buyers for a short period of time.

Six years ago, when my wife and I bought the house we live in now, it needed quite a bit of work, but we couldn't do any of that work until we owned the house. We were not in the position to buy it outright and so we had to sell our previous house in order to buy the new one.

The buyers of our old house were a young couple and first-time home buyers. They were still living with their parents so they had no problem renting our house back to us for two weeks while we did some remodeling on the new house. They got to lock in their interest rate and get their first mortgage payment paid by us. It was truly a win-win situation.

If that's not an option you might need to move into a temporary location. I know it's frustrating to move twice but if the deal is good enough it might be well worth it. If it's only for a short time you might be able to put your items in storage and take a vacation.

Get creative; you're homeless now. Have fun with it!

Conversely, maybe you're thinking you're going to buy a new place first.

If the market is that stiff and there's not much inventory out there this might make more sense. When you purchase the new home and still need to sell your old house, there are two types of contingencies we might use: the Home Sale Contingency or the Home Close Contingency.

The Home Close Contingency is the stronger of the two. This contingency says that you currently have a contract for sale on your previous home that just needs to close before you can close on your new purchase.

The Home Sale Contingency says that you still need to find a buyer for your old home before you can close on the new sale. Many sellers will not accept this type of contingency; therefore this would not be the preferred option. As a seller yourself you can imagine this might make you nervous.

You will need to decide, do you really need to sell? Perhaps you can hold your house as a rental property.

*For a list of things to think about when deciding to rent your house, visit
http://www.SellingHousesExposed.com/bonus for more information on property management.

9

COVER SHEETS ON YOUR TPS REPORTS?

It isn't necessary to imagine the world ending in fire or ice. There are two other possibilities: one is paperwork, and the other is nostalgia.

~Frank Zappa

Another way to get overwhelmed in the sales process is by the number of contracts and forms there are. I'm going to briefly list everything we need to know about nearly every piece of paper you'll be dealing with and give you a brief description on what you'll be doing with them.

The order can vary, but one of the first things you'll see is the listing agreement.

This is the document that gives your broker permission to market your property for sale and under what terms. This is just between you and the brokerage and no one else will be accessing that contract. It will spell out what your broker is required to do for you as well as your role in the process.

With that you're going to complete some disclosure forms. In Illinois you're specifically required to have a property disclosure.

The property disclosure lists some common defects that are often found in a house. This is your opportunity to disclose any of which you are aware, as is required by law. If there is nothing to disclose then that is what you state and you sign it and date it. We provide this to any serious buyer.

Along with that, if your property was built before 1979, you need to complete a lead-based paint disclosure.

We also have disclosures regarding radon hazards and mold. I will provide these forms for you and you can complete them even if you have no knowledge of lead-based paint problems, radon or mold. You would still disclose that, in fact, you have no knowledge of any problems.

48

To get a jump start on the disclosure forms, download them now at
http://www.SellingHousesExposed.com/bonus

Hopefully the next form we are encountering is the purchase contract. The purchase contract indicates the terms of the sale, who the buyer is, what they are wanting to buy exactly, and under what terms, such as when we'll have the closing date, whether it's a cash offer or financing purchase, and there will be several contingencies you'll want to review.

We have an attorney review period. Within five business days after acceptance your attorney can either approve the contract or reject the contract for any reason other than price or propose some modifications.

We also have the mortgage contingencies if the buyer is needing to get a loan. They will have to get it and it'll take time to get that loan, but they have requirements they'll have to do to get the application started and under what terms are they going to buy.

There are various other contingencies and terms that aren't as common that are necessary to discuss with your broker.

There will be an inspection report. If the buyer conducts an inspection or if you conduct a pre-listing inspection the inspection will itemize a third party's analysis of the status of the property.

Any lender is going to order an appraisal. An appraisal is also a third party opinion of the price value of the property.

You'll provide to your buyer a plat of survey which outlines the boundaries of the property as well as any easements. This obviously doesn't apply to condos.

You are going to provide the buyer the deed.

The deed will have a long complication legal description that is more specific than just the address of the property. The deed is the document that transfers ownership from one party to another. There are various types of deeds and your agent and attorney will discuss which one is appropriate for your situation.

Then there is the title. The title is the list of everything that has ever happened with a piece of property whether it has changed ownership and the status of those liens and whether they've been cleared.

Finally at closing you're going to receive the HUD-1 settlement statement – the key line items of which state how much cash you will be receiving from the sale after all of the fees have been taken out.

*To look at some sample contracts, check out http://www.SellingHousesExposed.com/bonus and call me with any questions.

51

Brian T. Wolf

Get Your Bonuses at
http://www.SellingHousesExposed.com/bonus

10

REAL ESTATE ROSETTA STONE

I am very much afraid of definitions, and yet one is almost forced to make them. One must take care, too, not to be inhibited by them.

~Robert Delaunay

Here's a list of potential terms you may run across when you buy or sell a house.

> Adjustable rate mortgage
> Agency
> Agent / Broker / Realtor™
> Amortization
> Annual percentage rate

53

Appraisal
Asking price
Assessed value
Balloon payment
Bridge loan
Building codes
Closing
Closing costs
Commission
Comparables
Condominium
Contingency
Contract
Conventional mortgage
Counteroffer
CRV certificate of reasonable value
Curb appeal
Deed
Disclosure laws
Discount points
Down payment
Earnest money / escrow deposit
Easement
Equity
Escrow account
Fannie Mae
FHA insured mortgage
Final walkthrough
Firm commitment
Fixed rate mortgage

Foreclosure
Freddie Mac
Home inspection
Home warranty
Homeowner's policy
Lien
Loan-to-value ratio
Market value
Marketable title
Mortgage
Mortgage broker
Mortgage insurance premium
Mortgagee
Mortgagor
Multiple listing service
Origination fee
Personal property
PITI
Point
Prequalification
Principal
Private mortgage insurance
Promissory note
Proration
Real property
Refinancing
RESPA statement
ROI
Survey
Title

Title defect
Title insurance
Title search
VA mortgage
Variance
Zoning

And that's just "some" of the terms. As you can see, it can be quite confusing and to some, it even seems as if it were a different language.

Fortunately for you, you're reading this book.

Why so fortunate?

Because I'm going to break things down to what you really need to know.

In the interest of time and your sanity, I will NOT define every single word related to real estate and real estate transactions. You can find that in a dictionary.

Instead, in order to simplify things for you, I've taken the most important terms and put them into categories. I then highlight each term and walk you through a simple explanation of each.

So sit back, grab a cup of coffee, and continue reading what real estate terms you really need to know…"stripped down."

BROKERAGE TERMS

You may hear the terms Agent, Broker, and Realtor™, used seemingly interchangeably. There is a lot of overlap between the terms. Becoming an Agent, Broker, or Realtor™ requires a significant amount of training and education, as well as a State Regulated and Certified Licensing Exam. This ensures that any real estate professional you're working with is held to a high standard of quality and professionalism.

Please note though that not all **Agents** and **Brokers** are **Realtors™**, but, in Illinois at least, all **Realtors™** are **Brokers**.

Many states have two license types for real estate professionals*: **Agent** and **Broker**. To operate a real estate office one needs to hold a **Brokers License**. This typically requires more coursework and testing than an **Agents License**, but either can assist you with your typical real estate transaction.

The National Association of Realtors™ (NAR) is a professional organization for real estate licensees. Only members of NAR, who agree to be bound by our code of ethics, may call themselves **Realtors™**.

Another professional group a licensee would join is a local **Multiple Listing Service (MLS.)** The **MLS** provides cooperation among brokerages for sharing listings of properties for sale or rent in a given geographic area.

*Not Illinois. State regulations change regularly. Consult your state's licensing requirements for the most current information.

VALUATION TERMS

When determining the value of a property we must distinguish between the market value, the asking price, the appraised value, and the assessed value.

The only one of them that ultimately matters is the market value. And the only way to know for sure the market value is to market the property for sale and find a buyer.

The **Market Value** is the price a buyer is willing to pay AND the price at which the seller is willing to sell. If one or both parties are unwilling, there won't be a sale.

To find the right buyer, we have to set the **Asking Price**, which is the price we want to sell the house at, as close to market value as possible from the start. (This is explained in more detail in chapter 3, For What It's Worth.)

A house with a good curb appeal can typically command a higher price.

An **Appraisal** is a type of third party opinion of value performed by a licensed appraiser.

Typically, an appraiser will determine a property's value by walking through a property and determining its condition. They will also note any amenities, upgrades, and overall structure of the property.

They will then use this information compared to other properties to come up with an Appraised Value which can then be used to qualify for a loan.

An appraisal can be useful in determining the right asking price, but most appraisals cost money and your broker can provide a **Comparable Market Analysis** as part of his service before listing the house for sale.

The **Assessed Value** is determined by the county assessor for taxation purposes. It may be the market value though often it is only a fractional number.

Knowing these different values can help us get the most out of your house at time of sale.

LISTING TERMS

Your broker will make you aware of any **Disclosure Laws** in your area. Most sellers are required by law to disclose any known **Latent Material Defects, Mold issues, Lead Paint hazards**, etc.

It's customary for the seller of a single family home to provide a **plat of survey** of their property. This is just to verify the lot boundaries and any easements or encroachments. **Easements** are the right to use someone else's property.

Encroachments are a trespass on someone else's property without their consent.

Bottom line is that when you sell a property, you don't want to mistakenly conceal any major defects which can affect the property's value.

Full disclosure is usually the best policy as this can protect you from future legal action.

CONTRACT TERMS

When we have an accepted offer to purchase, we are said to be **Under Contract**. The **Contract** is the formal and legally binding document that outlines the specific property being sold and under what terms.

Usually, when a contract is submitted by a buyer, they will include some earnest money.

Earnest money is a deposit made by the buyer to show that they are serious about buying the property. This is typically 2% - 3% of the purchase price; however, if a buyer wants to show that they are very serious about the offer, they may make a much larger earnest money deposit.

Most contracts, at least initially, contain one or more contingencies that must be satisfied in order to get to a successful closing.

A **Contingency** is a clause in the contract that specifies an item that either the buyer or seller needs to address.

If it cannot be addressed to mutual benefit, the contract can be canceled and the buyer may be entitled to a refund of all or a portion of their earnest money. If all contingencies are satisfied and the buyer still does not follow through on the purchase, they would forfeit their earnest money.

Get Your Bonuses at
http://www.SellingHousesExposed.com/bonus

A home inspection is an example of a legitimate contingency clause.

A **home inspection** is typically paid by the buyer in order to have a licensed home inspector evaluate the property.

A home inspector will perform a detailed inspection of the property and look for safety concerns such as electrical safety and integrity, contaminations, plumbing concerns, foundation challenges, and more. They will then provide a detailed report of any findings - good or bad which the buyer can then use as a reference for the purchase.

Sometimes a home inspection doesn't matter because a house may be sold **"as-is."** This means that the seller isn't guaranteeing anything and the buyer is purchasing the home "as-is" with any faults or defects — and they're o.k. with that.

In other cases, the seller may provide a **home warranty** which guarantees the mechanicals such as the furnace and water heater for a period of time — typically 13 months.

FINANCING TERMS

In October 2013, Forbes magazine reported that nearly half of all homes were purchased with cash. While that number is pretty high, a majority of buyers still need to obtain a loan to buy a home.

This type of loan is called a **Mortgage Loan**. It is quite common to hear it referred to as simply a Mortgage. However the Mortgage is only one piece of the puzzle.

A **Mortgage** is the security for the loan.

The **Mortgagor** is the borrower, who provides the Mortgage to the **Mortgagee**, the bank, as a promise to repay the loan.

Since this is a book about selling your house we won't go into too much more detail about buyer financing.

Given the numbers from Forbes there's at least a 51% chance you've already been through the process. As a seller your main concern regarding buyer financing is whether they have been preapproved and whether they are seeking an FHA Insured loan.

When you enter into a contract to sell your property to a buyer subject to his/her ability to obtain financing, you take a risk by taking your home off the market while they apply for the loan.

If the loan falls through you will have lost at least 4-6 weeks with no recourse. To protect yourself against this we make sure that the buyer has obtained a **Preapproval** from a reputable lender before agreeing to the contract.

In this process, a Mortgage Broker or other Loan Officer will review the buyer's credit reports, income, and other factors to determine whether they will be able to get approved for a loan. There is nothing wrong with asking potential buyers to get preapproved with a lender you trust as long as they are free to get their loan with a lender of their own choosing.

A buyer seeking an **FHA Insured loan** could need some additional help through the process. The Federal Housing Administration (FHA) has certain standards that every house must meet and they must pass an inspection to qualify for FHA financing.

If the property is part of a Homeowners Association, the HOA may also need to be FHA approved (though not in every case — check with your real estate professional.)

Instead of using an FHA loan, I purchased my first home at age 27 using a VA loan.

I didn't know anything about real estate at the time and hadn't bothered to save anything for a down payment. All I had going for me was a decent income from my full time job and six years of service in the Illinois Air National Guard.

Fortunately, the US Department of Veterans Affairs offers loan guarantees for those of us who've served in the military.

My loan officer was able to step me through the process and took care of everything so I was able to buy a home with no down payment and a reasonable interest rate. I sold that place less than two years later for $40,000 more than I paid.

Where else can you get any kind of return on a zero cash investment?!

That's when I got hooked on real estate!

CLOSING TERMS

A **Closing** is a general term to describe the official act of buying or selling your home. This is where all the paperwork is filled out and signed.

The terms relating to the **Closing of Escrow** can be among the most unfamiliar to the average person, especially the words "Closing" and "Escrow."

As we discussed earlier, when there is an agreement for a sale between a buyer and a seller, the buyer makes an earnest money deposit. This "Opens" the Escrow, or accounting of all money and documents related to the sale.

Once all of the terms of the contract have been satisfied we can Close the Escrow and close the sale. This is where the seller grants the Deed to the property to the buyer. The **Deed** is the document that officially transfers ownership of the property from one person to another.

I mentioned documents that are collected during the escrow period.

Among the most important of these is all of the title work that is done.

The **Title** is the record of everything that has affected or can affect the ownership of the property, including past deeds, liens, and encumbrances.

Encumbrances are specific rights to a property, which can be either financial or non-financial.

Financial encumbrances include liens (like a Mortgage or a Mechanics Lien,) which usually need to be paid/satisfied before the sale completes.

Non-financial encumbrances include Easements which grant partial use of the property to a third party, such as a utility company.

During a closing, a Title Company is hired to perform a Title Search and to underwrite the Title Insurance policy.

The **Title Search** shows the status of the title.

If there are any defects or clouds on title, the parties' attorneys will decide how to proceed.

Once the title is cleared of liens, defects, or clouds, it is said to be **Clear and Marketable Title**, which is generally the way it should be transferred to a new buyer.

The buyer customarily pays for the **Title Insurance policy**, which protects him or her from any claims which may arise and were not discovered during the title search.

11

SO LONG, AND THANKS
FOR ALL THE FISH

Tell them I said something.
~ The last words of Pancho Villa

My name is Brian T. Wolf. I am a residential real estate broker with RE/MAX at Home based out of Rolling Meadows, a suburb of Chicago, Illinois. I **help people** buy and sell houses. My duty to you as a client is to put the most amount of money in your pocket at closing as possible. And I will fight tooth and nail to get that done.

I've written down in these pages many of the ways I accomplish that. Of course every situation is unique and this is only a starting point. To determine what is right for you, visit my website www.SellingHousesExposed.com and call or email me right away.

I will leave you with a final checklist for you to use to determine your readiness to sell Fast and for More Money!

Repairs

1. If it needs to be repaired, repair it! There are always little things throughout the house that you just get used to over time. You might not think they are a big deal but a buyer might think that if you're not taking care of the little things, what big things might you have neglected?

2. Check everywhere for loose wallpaper and peeling paint.

3. Large repairs: major systems should be in good working condition or else disclosed to a buyer ahead of time. If a buyer feels you have been honest about disclosing everything they can feel more comfortable offering a higher price.

Get Your Bonuses at
http://www.SellingHousesExposed.com/bonus

Cleaning

4. Every living space in the home must shine! First impression is everything.

5. This includes all windows, inside and out.

6. Steam clean all rugs and carpeting. Polish all hard surface floors.

7. All woodwork, especially kitchen and bath cabinets, should be polished.

8. Clean all lamps and light fixtures.

9. When painting or carpeting choose colors that will appeal to the most people. Don't just think about what you might like.

Space Management

10. Furniture should be arranged to make the space appear as roomy as possible. Whenever possible, remove large items and furniture from crowded rooms.

11. Collectibles should be packed away for their protection and to keep from distracting a buyer from the other features of the house. Dispose of any unneeded items.

12. Get rid of all clutter. Make a habit of organizing clothing and personal possessions each day in preparation for any last minute showings.

13. Pack away off-season clothing in preparation for your move.

14. Lots of light creates a sense of space. Open all drapes. Switch on all lights before showings. Replace non-working bulbs everywhere.

Atmosphere

15. Clean smells equal positive images in the buyer's mind. Be mindful of any odors from pets, cooking, cigarettes, etc.

16. The best method is to remove the source of any smell instead of covering it up. Otherwise invest in room and carpet deodorizers or air fresheners as necessary.

17. If you have carpet with pet urine, the only way to remove the smell is to rip up the carpeting and padding, and replace them. Don't hesitate to make this investment if it's preventing the sale of your house.

18. Cooking or smoking odors can be alleviated by having carpets and furniture cleaned, and dry cleaning drapes.

19. Wet towels in the dirty laundry should not be allowed to pile up. Mildew odors are another big turnoff.

20. Now that you've removed possibly offensive odors, add pleasurable ones. Scents correlating to positive responses include: baking bread, cinnamon, fresh flowers, among others.

Staging – Use lighting and color to emphasize the best features of your home.

21. Furniture showrooms and magazine ads can be a great source of inspiration and illustrate small details that make a room more appealing. A basket of firewood, a book open on a table, or even flowers in a vase, can all add a little something to a room.

22. Rooms that seem a little bland can be dramatically improved by simply adding a brightly colored blanket or pillow on a couch or chair.

23. If you have pictures of your yard or house from various seasons, select the ones that show off your home the best. Considering hanging them around the house at eye level.

24. Natural light is ideal, so let it all in when you can. Add lamps as needed.

73

The Exterior – Look through the eyes of a buyer. Touch up or repair any needed maintenance.

25. Again use color to attract. Flowers on the front steps, such as petunias, geraniums, or impatiens, can be very welcoming.

26. Selling in winter? Consider a wreath of dried flowers on the door.

27. Try more pots of flowers around a porch or deck.

28. Windows and doors should all be operable and serviceable.

29. This includes making sure all cracked/broken windows are replaced, and all panes are clean.

30. Repair any holes or tears in screens.

31. Locks should all be functional.

32. Inspect and replace missing or loose shingles.

33. Put out the "Welcome" mat — literally! Buy one if you don't already have one.

The Yard

34. Keep it mowed and raked. Hire a service if you have to.

35. Trees and bushes need to be shaped/pruned.

36. Your front walk is another place to add colorful flowers.

37. Stage an "outdoor living" space. Set a scene such as chairs and a picnic table with a red and white checked tablecloth. Add some plastic utensils, plates, and glasses, and a buyer might be tempted to join you for a BBQ!

The Driveway

38. Free from clutter, especially toys!

39. Remember first impressions are everything. There should be nothing about the driveway a buyer can criticize – especially stains or dirt, debris or weeds.

The Front Entry – Keep in mind, we're still talking about the first impression here.

40. Analyze your entrance and see what kind of impression you think a buyer would have.

41. A mirror in the right spot will make it look larger.

75

42. How is the flooring? Add a small rug to protect the area during showings.

43. The front coat closet must appear roomy. Remove all off-season clothing, but leave a few of the empty hangers. A pomander ball or bag of cedar chips will add a pleasant touch.

The Living Areas

44. Any fireplace(s) should be clean and swept. Keep a few logs for proper staging, or even have a fire going in the winter.

45. A colorful item on the mantel adds accent, but take care you don't go too far. You don't want a buyer to think you live in a country craft store.

46. Keep furniture to a minimum for the best flow of traffic throughout.

47. Do you have a cathedral ceiling or exposed beams? Remove dust and cobwebs, and then consider accent lighting.

48. Do you have a TV that dominates the room? If possible replace with a smaller television set until you move.

The Dining Room

49. Set the table and accent with an attractive centerpiece.

50. If your dining table has leaves, remove them. Can you move the table against a wall? Showcase a fewer number of chairs if possible.

The Kitchen – Kitchens and baths are still what sell the home.

51. Hide small appliances whenever possible. Avoid clutter!

52. Hide detergents, cleansers, sponges, etc., out of sight.

53. Clean, clean, clean! Sinks, counter-tops, appliances, cabinets, etc.

54. Don't forget the top of the refrigerator!

55. Create a scene: open cookbook, mixing bowl with a wire whisk, maybe even a basket of fruit. Use your imagination.

56. Again, fresh aromas can come into play here. Bake cookies, bread, or apple pie. No need to make it from scratch – frozen premixed recipes do just fine.

57. Alternatively, a bowl of lemons or limes on the counter in the summer will do when you don't want to use the oven.

58. Neat, clean, organized. Check all storage spaces: pantries, cabinets, drawers. Remove what you can and organize the rest.

59. Analyze your window treatments. Are they clean and updated? Would it look better without?

60. Set the table with bright placemats and a homey centerpiece.

The Laundry Room – Don't hide it. Dress it up and show it off!

61. Fresh paint would go a long way here.

62. Clean and organize closets and other storage.

63. All dirty laundry must remain out of sight.

64. Washer and dryer should be cleaned and shiny.

65. If there's enough space, consider a complementary throw rug.

The Stairways

66. Safety first! Ensure adequate lighting.

67. Keep them clutter-free.

68. Railings should be secured.

69. There should be no loose carpeting or runners.

The Bedrooms

70. They should appear as large as possible. Remove clutter and when painting use lighter colors.

71. If the master bedroom has a private bath, color coordinate the two to create a "suite" effect.

72. Closets should appear spacious. Remove off-season clothes and any items on the floor. Maximize shelf space.

73. Keep the closets and the clothes in them fresh and clean smelling.

74. Light and bright applies to the closets as well. Add battery operated lights if needed.

75. Explain the plan to your children to get them on board as well. Don't be afraid to offer incentives for them to keep their beds made and rooms picked up prior to showings.

76. Children's toys, clothes, and other items are not exempt from packing up. Every room needs to be clutter-free.

77. Wall-hangings such as posters should be considered for storage, especially those that are personal or unusual.

The Bathrooms

78. Dirty or worn shower curtains must be replaced. Caulking around tubs, showers, sinks, etc., needs to be clean and serviceable. Remove mildewy or worn bath decals.

79. Store all personal care products out of sight. Clean and clutter-free!

80. Leaky faucets are a no-no! Repair and clean off mineral deposits with vinegar.

81. Medicine cabinets, storage cabinets, and drawers, should all be organized and clean. Throw away anything you find that's been hiding for years.

82. Hanging towels should contrast the wall color. Neutral for bold walls or bright for neutral walls. It's ok to buy new towels or rugs – you can use them in your new home.

83. Clean and polish the floor. If that doesn't work, cover as large an area as possible with a clean rug.

84. Personalize and decorate. Use your best towels and guest soaps. Add a plant for that extra touch.

85. Subtle fragrances only. Just a hint.

The Garage

86. Sweep and wash the floor. Organized, clean, clutter-free (sound familiar?)

87. Empty garages look larger so remove any cars before buyers visit. Add light where you can.

88. If it's not going to your new home, donate it or throw it away. Everything else stored neatly in boxes away from the walls.

If you find you need some help with repairs on this list I can recommend a great handyman to help you whip these out in a weekend. Visit www.SellingHousesExposed.com to contact me for more information.

Appendix

Sample Documents

- Multi-Board Residential Real Estate Contract 5.0
- Property Disclosure
- Mold Disclosure
- Disclosure of Information on Radon Hazards
- Lead-based Paint and/or Lead-based Paint Hazards

Brian T. Wolf

 MULTI-BOARD RESIDENTIAL REAL ESTATE CONTRACT 5.0

1 **1. THE PARTIES:** Buyer and Seller are hereinafter referred to as the "Parties".

2 Buyer(s) (Please Print) _____

3 Seller(s) (Please Print) _____

4 **If Dual Agency applies, complete Optional Paragraph 41.**

5 **2. THE REAL ESTATE:** Real Estate shall be defined as the Property, all improvements, the fixtures and
6 Personal Property included therein. Seller agrees to convey to Buyer or to Buyer's designated grantee, the
7 Real Estate with the approximate lot size or acreage of _____ commonly known as:

8 _____
9 Address   City   State   Zip
10 _____
11 County   Unit # (if applicable)   Permanent Index Number(s) of Real Estate

12 **If Condo/Coop/Townhome Parking is Included:** # of space(s) ____; identified as Space(s) #_____;
13 *(check type)* ❑ deeded space ❑ limited common element ❑ assigned space.

14 **3. FIXTURES AND PERSONAL PROPERTY:** All of the fixtures and included Personal Property are owned by
15 Seller and to Seller's knowledge are in operating condition on the Date of Acceptance, unless otherwise
16 stated herein. Seller agrees to transfer to Buyer all fixtures, all heating, electrical, plumbing and well systems
17 together with the following items of Personal Property by Bill of Sale at Closing:
18 *[Check or enumerate applicable items]*
19 __ Refrigerator   __ Central Air Conditioning   __ Central Humidifier   __ Light Fixtures, as they exist
20 __ Oven/Range/Stove   __ Window Air Conditioners   __ Water Softener (owned)   __ Built-in or Attached Shelving
21 __ Microwave   __ Ceiling Fan(s)   __ Sump Pumps   __ All Window Treatments & Hardware
22 __ Dishwasher   __ Intercom System   __ Electronic or Media Air Filter __ Existing Storms & Screens
23 __ Garbage Disposal   __ TV Antenna System   __ Central Vac & Equipment   __ Fireplace Screens/Doors/Grates
24 __ Trash Compactor   __ Satellite Dish   __ Security Systems (owned)   __ Fireplace Gas Logs
25 __ Washer   __ Outdoor Shed   __ Garage Door Openers   __ Invisible Fence System, Collars & Box
26 __ Dryer   __ Planted Vegetation   with all Transmitters   __ Smoke Detectors
27 __ Attached Gas Grill   __ Outdoor Playsets   __ All Tacked Down Carpeting __ Carbon Monoxide Detectors
28 **Other items included:** _____
29 **Items NOT included:** _____
30 Seller warrants to Buyer that all fixtures, systems and Personal Property included in this Contract shall be in
31 operating condition at Possession, except: _____.
32 A system or item shall be deemed to be in operating condition if it performs the function for which it is
33 intended, regardless of age, and does not constitute a threat to health or safety.
34 **Home Warranty ❑ shall ❑ shall not be included at a Premium not to exceed $_____.**

35 **4. PURCHASE PRICE:** Purchase Price of $_____ shall be paid as follows: Initial earnest money
36 of $_____ by ❑ check, ❑ cash OR ❑ note due on _____, 20____ to be increased
37 to a total of $_____ by _____, 20____. The earnest money shall be held by the
38 *[check one]* ❑ Seller's Broker ❑ Buyer's Broker as "Escrowee", in trust for the mutual benefit of the Parties.
39 The balance of the Purchase Price, as adjusted by prorations, shall be paid at Closing by wire transfer of

Buyer Initial _____	Buyer Initial _____	Seller Initial _____	Seller Initial _____
Address _____			v5.0e

1

		Save	Print

40 funds, or by certified, cashier's, mortgage lender's or title company's check (provided that the title company's
41 check is guaranteed by a licensed title insurance company).

42 **5. CLOSING:** Closing or escrow payout shall be on _____, 20___ or at such time as mutually
43 agreed by the Parties in writing. Closing shall take place at the escrow office of the title company (or its
44 issuing agent) that will issue the Owner's Policy of Title Insurance, situated nearest the Real Estate or as shall
45 be agreed mutually by the Parties.

46 **6. POSSESSION:** Unless otherwise provided in Paragraph 39, Seller shall deliver possession to Buyer at the
47 time of Closing. Possession shall be deemed to have been delivered when Seller has vacated the Real Estate
48 and delivered keys to the Real Estate to Buyer or to the office of the Seller's Broker.

49 **7. STATUTORY DISCLOSURES:** If applicable, prior to signing this Contract, Buyer *[check one]* ❏ has ❏ has
50 not received a completed Illinois Residential Real Property Disclosure Report; *[check one]* ❏ has ❏ has not
51 received the EPA Pamphlet, "Protect Your Family From Lead in Your Home"; *[check one]* ❏ has ❏ has not
52 received a Lead-Based Paint Disclosure; *[check one]* ❏ has ❏ has not received the IEMA Pamphlet "Radon
53 Testing Guidelines for Real Estate Transactions"; *[check one]* ❏ has ❏ has not received the Disclosure of
54 Information on Radon Hazards.

55 **8. PRORATIONS:** Proratable items shall include, without limitation, rents and deposits (if any) from tenants;
56 Special Service Area or Special Assessment Area tax for the year of Closing only; utilities, water and sewer;
57 and Homeowner or Condominium Association fees (and Master/Umbrella Association fees, if applicable).
58 Accumulated reserves of a Homeowner/Condominium Association(s) are not a proratable item. Seller
59 represents that as of the Date of Acceptance Homeowner/Condominium Association(s) fees are $_____
60 per _____ (and, if applicable, Master/Umbrella Association fees are $_____ per _____). Seller agrees
61 to pay prior to or at Closing any special assessments (by any association or governmental entity) confirmed
62 prior to the Date of Acceptance. Installments due after the year of Closing for a Special Assessment Area or
63 Special Service Area shall not be a proratable item and shall be payable by Buyer. The general Real Estate
64 taxes shall be prorated as of the date of Closing based on _____% of the most recent ascertainable full year
65 tax bill. All prorations shall be final as of Closing, except as provided in Paragraph 20. If the amount of the
66 most recent ascertainable full year tax bill reflects a homeowner, senior citizen or other exemption, a senior
67 freeze or senior deferral, then Seller has submitted or will submit in a timely manner all necessary
68 documentation to the appropriate governmental entity, before or after Closing, to preserve said exemption(s).

69 **9. ATTORNEY REVIEW:** Within five (5) Business Days after the Date of Acceptance, the attorneys for the
70 respective Parties, by Notice, may:
71 (a) Approve this Contract; or
72 (b) Disapprove this Contract, which disapproval shall not be based solely upon the Purchase Price; or
73 (c) Propose modifications except for the Purchase Price. If within ten (10) Business Days after the Date of
74   Acceptance written agreement is not reached by the Parties with respect to resolution of the proposed
75   modifications, then either Party may terminate this Contract by serving Notice, whereupon this Contract
76   shall be null and void; or
77 (d) Propose suggested changes to this Contract. If such suggestions are not agreed upon, neither Party may
78   declare this Contract null and void and this Contract shall remain in full force and effect.
79 **Unless otherwise specified, all Notices shall be deemed made pursuant to Paragraph 9(c). If Notice is not**
80 **served within the time specified herein, the provisions of this paragraph shall be deemed waived by the**
81 **Parties and this Contract shall remain in full force and effect.**

Buyer Initial _____	Buyer Initial _____	Seller Initial _____	Seller Initial _____
Address _____			v5.0e

82 **10. PROFESSIONAL INSPECTIONS AND INSPECTION NOTICES:** Buyer may conduct at Buyer's expense
83 (unless otherwise provided by governmental regulations) a home, radon, environmental, lead-based paint
84 and/or lead-based paint hazards (unless separately waived), and/or wood destroying insect infestation
85 inspection of the Real Estate by one or more licensed or certified inspection service(s).
86 (a) Buyer agrees that minor repairs and routine maintenance items of the Real Estate do not constitute
87 defects and are not a part of this contingency. **The fact that a functioning major component may be at**
88 **the end of its useful life shall not render such component defective for purposes of this paragraph.**
89 Buyer shall indemnify Seller and hold Seller harmless from and against any loss or damage caused by the
90 acts or negligence of Buyer or any person performing any inspection. The home inspection shall cover
91 only the major components of the Real Estate, including but not limited to central heating system(s),
92 central cooling system(s), plumbing and well system, electrical system, roof, walls, windows, ceilings,
93 floors, appliances and foundation. A major component shall be deemed to be in operating condition if it
94 performs the function for which it is intended, regardless of age, and does not constitute a threat to health
95 or safety. If radon mitigation is performed, Seller shall pay for any retest.
96 (b) Buyer shall serve Notice upon Seller or Seller's attorney of any defects disclosed by any inspection for
97 which Buyer requests resolution by Seller, together with a copy of the pertinent pages of the inspection
98 reports within five (5) Business Days (ten (10) calendar days for a lead-based paint and/or lead-based
99 paint hazard inspection) after the Date of Acceptance. If within ten (10) Business Days after the Date of
100 Acceptance written agreement is not reached by the Parties with respect to resolution of all inspection
101 issues, then either Party may terminate this Contract by serving Notice to the other Party, whereupon this
102 Contract shall be null and void.
103 (c) Notwithstanding anything to the contrary set forth above in this paragraph, in the event the inspection
104 reveals that the condition of the Real Estate is unacceptable to Buyer and Buyer serves Notice to Seller
105 within five (5) Business Days after the Date of Acceptance, this Contract shall be null and void.
106 (d) Failure of Buyer to conduct said inspection(s) and notify Seller within the time specified operates as a
107 waiver of Buyer's right to terminate this Contract under this Paragraph 10 and this Contract shall remain
108 in full force and effect.

109 **11. MORTGAGE CONTINGENCY:** This Contract is contingent upon Buyer obtaining a firm written mortgage
110 commitment (except for matters of title and survey or matters totally within Buyer's control) on or before
111 _____, 20____ for a *[check one]* ❏ fixed ❏ adjustable; *[check one]* ❏ conventional ❏ FHA/VA
112 (if FHA/VA is chosen, complete Paragraph 35) ❏ other_____ loan of ____% of Purchase
113 Price, plus private mortgage insurance (PMI), if required. The interest rate (initial rate, if applicable) shall not
114 exceed ____% per annum, amortized over not less than ____ years. Buyer shall pay loan origination fee
115 and/or discount points not to exceed ____% of the loan amount. Buyer shall pay the cost of application,
116 usual and customary processing fees and closing costs charged by lender. (Complete Paragraph 33 if closing
117 cost credits apply.) Buyer shall make written loan application within five (5) Business Days after the Date of
118 Acceptance. **Failure to do so shall constitute an act of Default under this Contract. If Buyer, having applied**
119 **for the loan specified above, is unable to obtain such loan commitment and serves Notice to Seller within**
120 **the time specified, this Contract shall be null and void. If Notice of inability to obtain such loan**
121 **commitment is not served within the time specified, Buyer shall be deemed to have waived this**
122 **contingency and this Contract shall remain in full force and effect. Unless otherwise provided in**
123 **Paragraph 31, this Contract shall not be contingent upon the sale and/or closing of Buyer's existing real**
124 **estate.** Buyer shall be deemed to have satisfied the financing conditions of this paragraph if Buyer obtains a
125 loan commitment in accordance with the terms of this paragraph even though the loan is conditioned on the
126 sale and/or closing of Buyer's existing real estate. If Seller at Seller's option and expense, within thirty (30)
127 days after Buyer's Notice, procures for Buyer such commitment or notifies Buyer that Seller will accept a

Buyer Initial _____ Buyer Initial _____ Seller Initial _____ Seller Initial _____
Address _____ v5.0e

3

86

128 purchase money mortgage upon the same terms, this Contract shall remain in full force and effect. In such
129 event, Seller shall notify Buyer within five (5) Business Days after Buyer's Notice of Seller's election to
130 provide or obtain such financing, and Buyer shall furnish to Seller or lender all requested information and
131 shall sign all papers necessary to obtain the mortgage commitment and to close the loan.

132 **12. HOMEOWNER INSURANCE:** This Contract is contingent upon Buyer obtaining evidence of insurability for
133 an Insurance Service Organization HO-3 or equivalent policy at standard premium rates within ten (10)
134 Business Days after the Date of Acceptance. **If Buyer is unable to obtain evidence of insurability and serves**
135 **Notice with proof of same to Seller within the time specified, this Contract shall be null and void. If**
136 **Notice is not served within the time specified, Buyer shall be deemed to have waived this contingency**
137 **and this Contract shall remain in full force and effect.**

138 **13. FLOOD INSURANCE:** Unless previously disclosed in the Illinois Residential Real Property Disclosure
139 Report, Buyer shall have the option to declare this Contract null and void if the Real Estate is located in a
140 special flood hazard area which requires Buyer to carry flood insurance. **If Notice of the option to declare**
141 **this Contract null and void is not given to Seller within ten (10) Business Days after the Date of**
142 **Acceptance or by the Mortgage Contingency deadline date described in Paragraph 11 (whichever is later),**
143 **Buyer shall be deemed to have waived such option and this Contract shall remain in full force and effect.**
144 Nothing herein shall be deemed to affect any rights afforded by the Residential Real Property Disclosure Act.

145 **14. CONDOMINIUM/COMMON INTEREST ASSOCIATIONS:** (If applicable) The Parties agree that the terms
146 contained in this paragraph, which may be contrary to other terms of this Contract, shall supersede any
147 conflicting terms.
148 (a) Title when conveyed shall be good and merchantable, subject to terms, provisions, covenants and
149 conditions of the Declaration of Condominium/Covenants, Conditions and Restrictions and all
150 amendments; public and utility easements including any easements established by or implied from the
151 Declaration of Condominium/Covenants, Conditions and Restrictions or amendments thereto; party wall
152 rights and agreements; limitations and conditions imposed by the Condominium Property Act;
153 installments due after the date of Closing of general assessments established pursuant to the Declaration
154 of Condominium/Covenants, Conditions and Restrictions.
155 (b) Seller shall be responsible for payment of all regular assessments due and levied prior to Closing and for
156 all special assessments confirmed prior to the Date of Acceptance.
157 (c) Buyer has, within five (5) Business Days from the Date of Acceptance, the right to demand from Seller
158 items as stipulated by the Illinois Condominium Property Act, if applicable, and Seller shall diligently
159 apply for same. This Contract is subject to the condition that Seller be able to procure and provide to
160 Buyer, a release or waiver of any option of first refusal or other pre-emptive rights of purchase created by
161 the Declaration of Condominium/Covenants, Conditions and Restrictions within the time established by
162 the Declaration of Condominium/Covenants, Conditions and Restrictions. In the event the
163 Condominium Association requires the personal appearance of Buyer and/or additional documentation,
164 Buyer agrees to comply with same.
165 (d) In the event the documents and information provided by Seller to Buyer disclose that the existing
166 improvements are in violation of existing rules, regulations or other restrictions or that the terms and
167 conditions contained within the documents would unreasonably restrict Buyer's use of the premises or
168 would result in financial obligations unacceptable to Buyer in connection with owning the Real Estate,
169 then Buyer may declare this Contract null and void by giving Seller Notice within five (5) Business Days
170 after the receipt of the documents and information required by Paragraph 14(c), listing those deficiencies
171 which are unacceptable to Buyer. If Notice is not served within the time specified, Buyer shall be deemed
172 to have waived this contingency, and this Contract shall remain in full force and effect.

Buyer Initial _____ *Buyer Initial* _____ *Seller Initial* _____ *Seller Initial* _____
Address _____ v5.0e

4

87

Brian T. Wolf

Save   Print

173 (e) Seller shall not be obligated to provide a condominium survey.
174 (f) Seller shall provide a certificate of insurance showing Buyer and Buyer's mortgagee, if any, as an insured.

175 **15. THE DEED:** Seller shall convey or cause to be conveyed to Buyer or Buyer's designated grantee good and
176 merchantable title to the Real Estate by recordable general Warranty Deed, with release of homestead rights,
177 (or the appropriate deed if title is in trust or in an estate), and with real estate transfer stamps to be paid by
178 Seller (unless otherwise designated by local ordinance). Title when conveyed will be good and merchantable,
179 subject only to: general real estate taxes not due and payable at the time of Closing; covenants, conditions
180 and restrictions of record; and building lines and easements, if any, provided they do not interfere with the
181 current use and enjoyment of the Real Estate.

182 **16. TITLE:** At Seller's expense, Seller will deliver or cause to be delivered to Buyer or Buyer's attorney within
183 customary time limitations and sufficiently in advance of Closing, as evidence of title in Seller or Grantor, a
184 title commitment for an ALTA title insurance policy in the amount of the Purchase Price with extended
185 coverage by a title company licensed to operate in the State of Illinois, issued on or subsequent to the Date of
186 Acceptance, subject only to items listed in Paragraph 15. The requirement to provide extended coverage shall
187 not apply if the Real Estate is vacant land. The commitment for title insurance furnished by Seller will be
188 conclusive evidence of good and merchantable title as therein shown, subject only to the exceptions therein
189 stated. **If the title commitment discloses any unpermitted exceptions or if the Plat of Survey shows any**
190 **encroachments or other survey matters that are not acceptable to Buyer, then Seller shall have said**
191 **exceptions, survey matters or encroachments removed, or have the title insurer commit to either insure**
192 **against loss or damage that may result from such exceptions or survey matters or insure against any court-**
193 **ordered removal of the encroachments.** If Seller fails to have such exceptions waived or insured over prior to
194 Closing, Buyer may elect to take the title as it then is with the right to deduct from the Purchase Price prior
195 encumbrances of a definite or ascertainable amount. Seller shall furnish Buyer at Closing an Affidavit of Title
196 covering the date of Closing, and shall sign any other customary forms required for issuance of an ALTA
197 Insurance Policy.

198 **17. PLAT OF SURVEY:** Not less than one (1) Business Day prior to Closing, except where the Real Estate is a
199 condominium (see Paragraph 14) Seller shall, at Seller's expense, furnish to Buyer or Buyer's attorney a Plat
200 of Survey that conforms to the current Minimum Standards of Practice for boundary surveys, is dated not
201 more than six (6) months prior to the date of Closing, and is prepared by a professional land surveyor
202 licensed to practice land surveying under the laws of the State of Illinois. The Plat of Survey shall show
203 visible evidence of improvements, rights of way, easements, use and measurements of all parcel lines. The
204 land surveyor shall set monuments or witness corners at all accessible corners of the land. All such corners
205 shall also be visibly staked or flagged. The Plat of Survey shall include the following statement placed near
206 the professional land surveyor seal and signature: "This professional service conforms to the current Illinois
207 Minimum Standards for a boundary survey." A Mortgage Inspection, as defined, is not a boundary survey
208 and is not acceptable.

209 **18. ESCROW CLOSING:** At the election of either Party, not less than five (5) Business Days prior to Closing,
210 this sale shall be closed through an escrow with the lending institution or the title company in accordance
211 with the provisions of the usual form of Deed and Money Escrow Agreement, as agreed upon between the
212 Parties, with provisions inserted in the Escrow Agreement as may be required to conform with this Contract.
213 The cost of the escrow shall be paid by the Party requesting the escrow. If this transaction is a cash purchase
214 (no mortgage is secured by Buyer), the Parties shall share the title company escrow closing fee equally.

215 **19. DAMAGE TO REAL ESTATE OR CONDEMNATION PRIOR TO CLOSING:** If prior to delivery of the deed the
216 Real Estate shall be destroyed or materially damaged by fire or other casualty, or the Real Estate is taken by

Buyer Initial _____ *Buyer Initial* _____ *Seller Initial* _____ *Seller Initial* _____

Address _____ v5.0e

5

88

Get Your Bonuses at
http://www.SellingHousesExposed.com/bonus

217 condemnation, then Buyer shall have the option of either terminating this Contract (and receiving a refund of
218 earnest money) or accepting the Real Estate as damaged or destroyed, together with the proceeds of the
219 condemnation award or any insurance payable as a result of the destruction or damage, which gross
220 proceeds Seller agrees to assign to Buyer and deliver to Buyer at Closing. Seller shall not be obligated to
221 repair or replace damaged improvements. The provisions of the Uniform Vendor and Purchaser Risk Act of
222 the State of Illinois shall be applicable to this Contract, except as modified by this paragraph.

223 **20. REAL ESTATE TAX ESCROW:** In the event the Real Estate is improved, but has not been previously taxed
224 for the entire year as currently improved, the sum of three percent (3%) of the Purchase Price shall be
225 deposited in escrow with the title company with the cost of the escrow to be divided equally by Buyer and
226 Seller and paid at Closing. When the exact amount of the taxes to be prorated under this Contract can be
227 ascertained, the taxes shall be prorated by Seller's attorney at the request of either Party and Seller's share of
228 such tax liability after proration shall be paid to Buyer from the escrow funds and the balance, if any, shall be
229 paid to Seller. If Seller's obligation after such proration exceeds the amount of the escrow funds, Seller agrees
230 to pay such excess promptly upon demand.

231 **21. SELLER REPRESENTATIONS:** Seller represents that with respect to the Real Estate Seller has no
232 knowledge of nor has Seller received written notice from any governmental body regarding:
233 (a) zoning, building, fire or health code violations that have not been corrected;
234 (b) any pending rezoning;
235 (c) boundary line disputes;
236 (d) any pending condemnation or Eminent Domain proceeding;
237 (e) easements or claims of easements not shown on the public records;
238 (f) any hazardous waste on the Real Estate;
239 (g) any improvements to the Real Estate for which the required permits were not obtained;
240 (h) any improvements to the Real Estate which are not included in full in the determination of the most
241 recent tax assessment; or
242 (i) any improvements to the Real Estate which are eligible for the home improvement tax exemption.

243 Seller further represents that:
244 1. There [check one] ❑ is ❑ is not a pending or unconfirmed special assessment affecting the Real Estate by
245 any association or governmental entity payable by Buyer after date of Closing.
246 2. The Real Estate [check one] ❑ is ❑ is not located within a Special Assessment Area or Special Service
247 Area, payments for which will not be the obligation of Seller after the year in which the Closing occurs.
248 **If any of the representations contained herein regarding a Special Assessment Area or Special Service
249 Area are unacceptable to Buyer, Buyer shall have the option to declare this Contract null and void. If
250 Notice of the option to declare this Contract null and void is not given to Seller within ten (10) Business
251 Days after the Date of Acceptance or by the Mortgage Contingency deadline date described in Paragraph
252 11 (whichever is later), Buyer shall be deemed to have waived such option and this Contract shall remain
253 in full force and effect. Seller's representations contained in this paragraph shall survive the Closing.**

254 **22. CONDITION OF REAL ESTATE AND INSPECTION:** Seller agrees to leave the Real Estate in broom clean
255 condition. All refuse and personal property that is not to be conveyed to Buyer shall be removed from the
256 Real Estate at Seller's expense prior to delivery of Possession. Buyer shall have the right to inspect the Real
257 Estate, fixtures and included Personal Property prior to Possession to verify that the Real Estate,
258 improvements and included Personal Property are in substantially the same condition as of the Date of
259 Acceptance, normal wear and tear excepted.

Buyer Initial _____ Buyer Initial _____ Seller Initial _____ Seller Initial _____
Address _____ v5.0

6

89

Get Your Bonuses at
http://www.SellingHousesExposed.com/bonus

23. MUNICIPAL ORDINANCE, TRANSFER TAX, AND GOVERNMENTAL COMPLIANCE:

(a) Parties are cautioned that the Real Estate may be situated in a municipality that has adopted a pre-closing inspection requirement, municipal Transfer Tax or other similar ordinances. Transfer taxes required by municipal ordinance shall be paid by the party designated in such ordinance.

(b) Parties agree to comply with the reporting requirements of the applicable sections of the Internal Revenue Code and the Real Estate Settlement Procedures Act of 1974, as amended.

24. BUSINESS DAYS/HOURS: Business Days are defined as Monday through Friday, excluding Federal holidays. Business Hours are defined as 8:00 A.M. to 6:00 P.M. Chicago time.

25. FACSIMILE OR DIGITAL SIGNATURES: Facsimile or digital signatures shall be sufficient for purposes of executing, negotiating, and finalizing this Contract.

26. DIRECTION TO ESCROWEE: In every instance where this Contract shall be deemed null and void or if this Contract may be terminated by either Party, the following shall be deemed incorporated: "and earnest money refunded to Buyer upon written direction of the Parties to Escrowee or upon entry of an order by a court of competent jurisdiction". There shall be no disbursement of earnest money unless Escrowee has been provided written direction from Seller and Buyer. Absent a direction relative to the disbursement of earnest money within a reasonable period of time, Escrowee may deposit funds with the Clerk of the Circuit Court by the filing of an action in the nature of Interpleader. Escrowee shall be reimbursed from the earnest money for all costs, including reasonable attorney fees, related to the filing of the Interpleader action. Seller and Buyer shall indemnify and hold Escrowee harmless from any and all conflicting claims and demands arising under this paragraph.

27. NOTICE: Except as provided in Paragraph 31(C)(2) regarding the manner of service for "kick-out" Notices, all Notices shall be in writing and shall be served by one Party or attorney to the other Party or attorney. Notice to any one of a multiple person Party shall be sufficient Notice to all. Notice shall be given in the following manner:

(a) By personal delivery; or

(b) By mailing to the addresses recited herein by regular mail and by certified mail, return receipt requested. Except as otherwise provided herein, Notice served by certified mail shall be effective on the date of mailing; or

(c) By facsimile transmission. Notice shall be effective as of date and time of the transmission, provided that the Notice transmitted shall be sent on Business Days during Business Hours. In the event Notice is transmitted during non-business hours, the effective date and time of Notice is the first hour of the next Business Day after transmission; or

(d) By e-mail transmission if an e-mail address has been furnished by the recipient Party or the recipient Party's attorney to the sending Party or is shown on this Contract. Notice shall be effective as of date and time of e-mail transmission, provided that, in the event e-mail Notice is transmitted during non-business hours, the effective date and time of Notice is the first hour of the next Business Day after transmission. An attorney or Party may opt out of future e-mail Notice by any form of Notice provided by this Contract; or

(e) By commercial overnight delivery (e.g., FedEx). Such Notice shall be effective on the next Business Day following deposit with the overnight delivery company.

28. PERFORMANCE: Time is of the essence of this Contract. In any action with respect to this Contract, the Parties are free to pursue any legal remedies at law or in equity and the prevailing Party in litigation shall be entitled to collect reasonable attorney fees and costs from the non-Prevailing Party as ordered by a court of competent jurisdiction.

| Buyer Initial _____ | Buyer Initial _____ | Seller Initial _____ | Seller Initial _____ |

Address _____   v5.0

7

90

| Save | Print |

304 **29. CHOICE OF LAW/GOOD FAITH:** All terms and provisions of this Contract including but not limited to the
305 Attorney Review and Professional Inspection Paragraphs shall be governed by the laws of the State of Illinois
306 and are subject to the covenant of good faith and fair dealing implied in all Illinois contracts.

307 **30. OTHER PROVISIONS:** This Contract is also subject to those OPTIONAL PROVISIONS initialed by the
308 Parties and the following attachments, if any: _____
309 _____.

310 **OPTIONAL PROVISIONS (Applicable ONLY if initialed by all Parties)**

311 ____ ____ ____ ____ **31. SALE OF BUYER'S REAL ESTATE:**
312 [Initials]
313 **(A) REPRESENTATIONS ABOUT BUYER'S REAL ESTATE:** Buyer represents to Seller as follows:
314   (1) Buyer owns real estate commonly known as (address):
315 _____.
316   (2) Buyer *[check one]* ❑ has ❑ has not entered into a contract to sell said real estate.
317   If Buyer has entered into a contract to sell said real estate, that contract:
318   (a) *[check one]* ❑ is ❑ is not subject to a mortgage contingency.
319   (b) *[check one]* ❑ is ❑ is not subject to a real estate sale contingency.
320   (c) *[check one]* ❑ is ❑ is not subject to a real estate closing contingency.
321   (3) Buyer *[check one]* ❑ has ❑ has not listed said real estate for sale with a licensed real estate broker and
322   in a local multiple listing service.
323   (4) If Buyer's real estate is not listed for sale with a licensed real estate broker and in a local multiple
324   listing service, Buyer *[check one]*
325   (a) ❑ Shall list said real estate for sale with a licensed real estate broker who will place it in a local
326   multiple listing service within five (5) Business Days after the Date of Acceptance.
327   [For information only] Broker: _____
328   Broker's Address: _____ Phone: _____.
329   (b) ❑ Does not intend to list said real estate for sale.
330 **(B) CONTINGENCIES BASED UPON SALE AND/OR CLOSE OF BUYER'S REAL ESTATE:**
331   (1) This Contract is contingent upon Buyer having entered into a contract for the sale of Buyer's real
332   estate that is in full force and effect as of _____, 20____. Such contract should provide
333   for a closing date not later than the Closing Date set forth in this Contract. **If Notice is served on or**
334   **before the date set forth in this subparagraph that Buyer has not procured a contract for the sale of**
335   **Buyer's real estate, this Contract shall be null and void. If Notice that Buyer has not procured a**
336   **contract for the sale of Buyer's real estate is not served on or before the close of business on the**
337   **date set forth in this subparagraph, Buyer shall be deemed to have waived all contingencies**
338   **contained in this Paragraph 31, and this Contract shall remain in full force and effect.** (If this
339   paragraph is used, then the following paragraph **must** be completed.)
340   (2) In the event Buyer has entered into a contract for the sale of Buyer's real estate as set forth in
341   Paragraph 31(B)(1) and that contract is in full force and effect, or has entered into a contract for the
342   sale of Buyer's real estate prior to the execution of this Contract, this Contract is contingent upon
343   Buyer closing the sale of Buyer's real estate on or before _____, 20____. **If Notice that**
344   **Buyer has not closed the sale of Buyer's real estate is served before the close of business on the**
345   **next Business Day after the date set forth in the preceding sentence, this Contract shall be null and**
346   **void. If Notice is not served as described in the preceding sentence, Buyer shall be deemed to have**
347   **waived all contingencies contained in this Paragraph 31, and this Contract shall remain in full**
348   **force and effect.**

Buyer Initial _____ *Buyer Initial* _____ *Seller Initial* _____ *Seller Initial* _____
Address _____ v5.0

8

91

Get Your Bonuses at
http://www.SellingHousesExposed.com/bonus

Brian T. Wolf

| Save | Print |

349 (3) If the contract for the sale of Buyer's real estate is terminated for any reason after the date set forth in
350 Paragraph 31(B)(1) (or after the date of this Contract if no date is set forth in Paragraph 31(B)(1)),
351 Buyer shall, within three (3) Business Days of such termination, notify Seller of said termination.
352 **Unless Buyer, as part of said Notice, waives all contingencies in Paragraph 31 and complies with**
353 **Paragraph 31(D), this Contract shall be null and void as of the date of Notice. If Notice as required**
354 **by this subparagraph is not served within the time specified, Buyer shall be in default under the**
355 **terms of this Contract.**
356 **(C) SELLER'S RIGHT TO CONTINUE TO OFFER REAL ESTATE FOR SALE**: During the time of this contingency,
357 Seller has the right to continue to show the Real Estate and offer it for sale subject to the following:
358 (1) If Seller accepts another bona fide offer to purchase the Real Estate while the contingencies expressed
359 in Paragraph 31(B) are in effect, Seller shall notify Buyer in writing of same. Buyer shall then have
360 _____ hours after Seller gives such Notice to waive the contingencies set forth in Paragraph
361 31(B), subject to Paragraph 31(D).
362 (2) Seller's Notice to Buyer (commonly referred to as a 'kick-out' Notice) shall be in writing and shall be
363 served on Buyer, not Buyer's attorney or Buyer's real estate agent. Courtesy copies of such "kick-out"
364 Notice should be sent to Buyer's attorney and Buyer's real estate agent, if known. Failure to provide
365 such courtesy copies shall not render Notice invalid. Notice to any one of a multiple-person Buyer
366 shall be sufficient Notice to all Buyers. Notice for the purpose of this subparagraph only shall be
367 served upon Buyer in the following manner:
368 (a) By personal delivery effective at the time and date of personal delivery; or
369 (b) By mailing to the addresses recited herein for Buyer by regular mail and by certified mail. Notice
370 shall be effective at 10:00 A.M. on the morning of the second day following deposit of Notice in
371 the U.S. Mail; or
372 (c) By commercial overnight delivery (e.g., FedEx). Notice shall be effective upon delivery or at 4:00
373 P.M. Chicago time on the next delivery day following deposit with the overnight delivery
374 company, whichever first occurs.
375 (3) If Buyer complies with the provisions of Paragraph 31(D) then this Contract shall remain in full force
376 and effect.
377 (4) If the contingencies set forth in Paragraph 31(B) are NOT waived in writing within said time period
378 by Buyer, this Contract shall be null and void.
379 (5) Except as provided in Paragraph 31(C)(2) above, all Notices shall be made in the manner provided by
380 Paragraph 27 of this Contract.
381 (6) Buyer waives any ethical objection to the delivery of Notice under this paragraph by Seller's attorney
382 or representative.
383 **(D) WAIVER OF PARAGRAPH 31 CONTINGENCIES**: Buyer shall be deemed to have waived the contingencies in
384 Paragraph 31(B) when Buyer has delivered written waiver and deposited with the Escrowee additional
385 earnest money in the amount of $_____ in the form of a cashier's or certified check within the
386 time specified. **If Buyer fails to deposit the additional earnest money within the time specified, the waiver**
387 **shall be deemed ineffective and this Contract shall be null and void.**
388 **(E) BUYER COOPERATION REQUIRED:** Buyer authorizes Seller or Seller's agent to verify representations
389 contained in Paragraph 31 at any time, and Buyer agrees to cooperate in providing relevant information.

390 ___ ___ ___ ___ **32. CANCELLATION OF PRIOR REAL ESTATE CONTRACT:** In the event either Party has
391 entered into a prior real estate contract, this Contract shall be subject to written cancellation of the prior
392 contract on or before _____, 20___. **In the event the prior contract is not cancelled within the**
393 **time specified, this Contract shall be null and void. Seller's notice to the purchaser under the prior**

| Buyer Initial _____ | Buyer Initial _____ | Seller Initial _____ | Seller Initial _____ |

Address _____ v5.0

9

92

Get Your Bonuses at
http://www.SellingHousesExposed.com/bonus

| Save | Print |

394 contract should not be served until after Attorney Review and Professional Inspections provisions of this
395 Contract have expired, been satisfied or waived.

396 ___ ___ ___ ___ **33. CREDIT AT CLOSING:** Provided Buyer's lender permits such credit to show on the
397 HUD-1 Settlement Statement, **and if not, such lesser amount as the lender permits,** Seller agrees to credit to
398 Buyer at Closing $_____ to be applied to prepaid expenses, closing costs or both.

399 ___ ___ ___ ___ **34. INTEREST BEARING ACCOUNT:** Earnest money (with a completed W-9 and other
400 required forms), shall be held in a federally insured interest bearing account at a financial institution
401 designated by Escrowee. All interest earned on the earnest money shall accrue to the benefit of and be paid to
402 Buyer. **Buyer shall be responsible for any administrative fee (not to exceed $100) charged for setting up the
403 account.** In anticipation of Closing, the Parties direct Escrowee to close the account no sooner than ten (10)
404 Business Days prior to the anticipated Closing date.

405 ___ ___ ___ ___ **35. VA OR FHA FINANCING:** If Buyer is seeking VA or FHA financing, this provision shall
406 be applicable: **Required FHA or VA amendments and disclosures shall be attached to this Contract.** If VA,
407 the Funding Fee, or if FHA, the Mortgage Insurance Premium (MIP) shall be paid by Buyer and *[check one]*
408 ❑ shall ❑ shall not be added to the mortgage loan amount.

409 ___ ___ ___ ___ **36. INTERIM FINANCING:** This Contract is contingent upon Buyer obtaining a written
410 commitment for interim financing on or before _____, 20___ in the amount of $_____.
411 **If Buyer is unable to secure the interim financing commitment and gives Notice to Seller within the time
412 specified, this Contract shall be null and void. If Notice is not served within the time specified, this
413 provision shall be deemed waived by the Parties and this Contract shall remain in full force and effect.**

414 ___ ___ ___ ___ **37. WELL AND/OR SEPTIC/SANITARY INSPECTIONS:** Seller shall obtain at Seller's
415 expense a well water test stating that the well delivers not less than five (5) gallons of water per minute and
416 including a bacteria and nitrate test (and lead test for FHA loans) and/or a septic report from the applicable
417 County Health Department, a Licensed Environmental Health Practitioner, or a licensed well and septic
418 inspector, each dated not more than ninety (90) days prior to Closing, stating that the well and water supply
419 and the private sanitary system are in proper operating condition with no defects noted. Seller shall remedy
420 any defect or deficiency disclosed by said report(s) prior to Closing, provided that if the cost of remedying a
421 defect or deficiency and the cost of landscaping together exceed $3,000.00, and if the Parties cannot reach
422 agreement regarding payment of such additional cost, this Contract may be terminated by either Party.
423 Additional testing recommended by the report shall be obtained at Seller's expense. If the report
424 recommends additional testing after Closing, the Parties shall have the option of establishing an escrow with
425 a mutual cost allocation for necessary repairs or replacements, or either Party may terminate this Contract
426 prior to Closing. Seller shall deliver a copy of such evaluation(s) to Buyer not less than one (1) Business Day
427 prior to Closing.

428 ___ ___ ___ ___ **38. WOOD DESTROYING INFESTATION:** Notwithstanding the provisions of Paragraph 10,
429 within ten (10) Business Days after the Date of Acceptance, Seller at Seller's expense shall deliver to Buyer a
430 written report, dated not more than six (6) months prior to the date of Closing, by a licensed inspector
431 certified by the appropriate state regulatory authority in the subcategory of termites, stating that there is no
432 visible evidence of active infestation by termites or other wood destroying insects. Unless otherwise agreed
433 between the Parties, if the report discloses evidence of active infestation or structural damage, Buyer has the
434 option within five (5) Business Days of receipt of the report to proceed with the purchase or declare this
435 Contract null and void.

Buyer Initial _____   *Buyer Initial* _____   *Seller Initial* _____   *Seller Initial* _____

Address _____   v5.0

10

93

Get Your Bonuses at
http://www.SellingHousesExposed.com/bonus

Brian T. Wolf

| | | Save | Print |

436 ____ ____ ____ ____ **39. POST-CLOSING POSSESSION:** Possession shall be delivered no later than 11:59 P.M.
437 on the date that is _____ days after the date of Closing ("the Possession Date"). Seller shall be responsible
438 for all utilities, contents said liability insurance, and home maintenance expenses until delivery of possession.
439 Seller shall deposit in escrow at Closing with _____, *[check one]* ❑ one percent (1%) of the
440 Purchase Price or ❑ the sum of $_____ to be paid by Escrowee as follows:
441 (a) The sum of $_____ per day for use and occupancy from and including the day after
442 Closing to and including the day of delivery of Possession, if on or before the Possession Date;
443 (b) The amount per day equal to three (3) times the daily amount set forth herein shall be paid for each day
444 after the Possession Date specified in this paragraph that Seller remains in possession of the Real Estate;
445 and
446 (c) The balance, if any, to Seller after delivery of Possession and provided that the terms of Paragraph 22
447 have been satisfied. Seller's liability under this paragraph shall not be limited to the amount of the
448 possession escrow deposit referred to above. Nothing herein shall be deemed to create a
449 Landlord/Tenant relationship between the Parties.

450 ____ ____ ____ ____ **40. "AS IS" CONDITION:** This Contract is for the sale and purchase of the Real Estate in its
451 "As Is" condition as of the Date of Offer. Buyer acknowledges that no representations, warranties or
452 guarantees with respect to the condition of the Real Estate have been made by Seller or Seller's Designated
453 Agent other than those known defects, if any, disclosed by Seller. Buyer may conduct an inspection at
454 Buyer's expense. In that event, Seller shall make the Real Estate available to Buyer's inspector at reasonable
455 times. Buyer shall indemnify Seller and hold Seller harmless from and against any loss or damage caused by
456 the acts or negligence of Buyer or any person performing any inspection. **In the event the inspection reveals**
457 **that the condition of the Real Estate is unacceptable to Buyer and Buyer so notifies Seller within five (5)**
458 **Business Days after the Date of Acceptance, this Contract shall be null and void. Failure of Buyer to notify**
459 **Seller or to conduct said inspection operates as a waiver of Buyer's right to terminate this Contract under**
460 **this paragraph and this Contract shall remain in full force and effect.** Buyer acknowledges that the
461 provisions of Paragraph 10 and the warranty provisions of Paragraph 3 do not apply to this Contract.

462 ____ ____ ____ ____ **41. CONFIRMATION OF DUAL AGENCY:** The Parties confirm that they have previously
463 consented to _____
464 (Licensee) acting as a Dual Agent in providing brokerage services on their behalf and specifically consent to
465 Licensee acting as a Dual Agent with regard to the transaction referred to in this Contract.

466 ____ ____ ____ ____ **42. SPECIFIED PARTY APPROVAL:** This Contract is contingent upon the approval of the
467 Real Estate by _____
468 Buyer's Specified Party, within five (5) Business Days after the Date of Acceptance. In the event Buyer's
469 Specified Party does not approve of the Real Estate and Notice is given to Seller within the time specified,
470 this Contract shall be null and void. If Notice is not served within the time specified, this provision shall be
471 deemed waived by the Parties and this Contract shall remain in full force and effect.

472 ____ ____ ____ ____ **43. MISCELLANEOUS PROVISIONS:** Buyer's and Seller's obligations are contingent upon
473 the Parties entering into a separate written agreement consistent with the terms and conditions set forth
474 herein, and with such additional terms as either Party may deem necessary, providing for one or more of the
475 following: *(check applicable boxes)*
476 ❑ Articles of Agreement for Deed or   ❑ Assumption of Seller's Mortgage   ❑ Commercial/Investment
477   Purchase Money Mortgage   ❑ Cooperative Apartment   ❑ New Construction
478 ❑ Short Sale   ❑ Tax-Deferred Exchange   ❑ Vacant Land

Buyer Initial _____ Buyer Initial _____ Seller Initial _____ Seller Initial _____
Address _____ v5.0

Get Your Bonuses at
http://www.SellingHousesExposed.com/bonus

479 **THIS DOCUMENT WILL BECOME A LEGALLY BINDING CONTRACT WHEN SIGNED BY ALL PARTIES AND**
480 **DELIVERED TO THE PARTIES OR THEIR AGENTS.**

481 The Parties represent that the text of this form has not been altered and is identical to the official Multi-Board
482 Residential Real Estate Contract 5.0.

483
484 Date of Offer | DATE OF ACCEPTANCE

485
486 Buyer Signature | Seller Signature

487
488 Buyer Signature | Seller Signature

489
490 Print Buyer(s) Name(s) *[Required]* | Print Seller(s) Name(s) *[Required]*

491
492 Address | Address

493
494 City · State · Zip | City · State · Zip

495
496 Phone · E-mail | Phone · E-mail

497 *FOR INFORMATION ONLY*

498
499 Buyer's Broker · MLS # | Seller's Broker · MLS #

500
501 Buyer's Designated Agent · MLS # | Seller's Designated Agent · MLS #

502
503 Phone · Fax | Phone · Fax

504
505 E-mail | E-mail

506
507 Buyer's Attorney · E-mail | Seller's Attorney · E-mail

508
509 Phone · Fax | Phone · Fax

510
511 Mortgage Company · Phone | Homeowner's/Condo Association (if any) · Phone

512
513 Loan Officer · Phone/Fax | Management Co. /Other Contact · Phone

514 ©2009, Illinois Real Estate Lawyers Association. All rights reserved. **Unauthorized duplication or alteration of this form or**
515 **any portion thereof is prohibited.** Official form available at www.irela.org (web site of Illinois Real Estate Lawyers
516 Association).

Approved by the following organizations as of July 20, 2009

517 Illinois Real Estate Lawyers Association · DuPage County Bar Association · Will County Bar Association
518 Northwest Suburban Bar Association · Chicago Association of REALTORS®
519 Mainstreet Organization of REALTORS® · Aurora-Tri County Association of REALTORS®· West Towns Board of REALTORS®
520 REALTOR® Association of Northwest Chicagoland · REALTOR® Association of the Fox Valley
521 Oak Park Area Association of REALTORS® · McHenry Association of REALTORS® · Three Rivers Association of REALTORS®
522 North Shore–Barrington Association of REALTORS®

523 **Seller Rejection:** This offer was presented to Seller on _____, 20____ at ____:____ AM/PM
524 and rejected on _____, 20____ at ____:____ AM/PM ____ ____ (Seller initials).

Buyer Initial _____ Buyer Initial _____ Seller Initial _____ Seller Initial _____
Address _____ v5.0

12

Get Your Bonuses at
http://www.SellingHousesExposed.com/bonus

Brian T. Wolf

Illinois Association of REALTORS®
RESIDENTIAL REAL PROPERTY DISCLOSURE REPORT

NOTICE: THE PURPOSE OF THIS REPORT IS TO PROVIDE PROSPECTIVE BUYERS WITH INFORMATION ABOUT MATERIAL DEFECTS IN THE RESIDENTIAL REAL PROPERTY. THIS REPORT DOES NOT LIMIT THE PARTIES RIGHT TO CONTRACT FOR THE SALE OF RESIDENTIAL REAL PROPERTY IN "AS IS" CONDITION. UNDER COMMON LAW SELLERS WHO DISCLOSE MATERIAL DEFECTS MAY BE UNDER A CONTINUING OBLIGATION TO ADVISE THE PROSPECTIVE BUYERS ABOUT THE CONDITION OF THE RESIDENTIAL REAL PROPERTY EVEN AFTER THE REPORT IS DELIVERED TO THE PROSPECTIVE BUYER. COMPLETION OF THIS REPORT BY SELLER CREATES LEGAL OBLIGATIONS ON SELLER THEREFORE SELLER MAY WISH TO CONSULT AN ATTORNEY PRIOR TO COMPLETION OF THIS REPORT.

Property Address: _____
City, State & Zip Code: _____
Seller's Name: _____

This report is a disclosure of certain conditions of the residential real property listed above in compliance with the Residential Real Property Disclosure Act. This information is provided as of _____, 20____, and does not reflect any changes made or occurring after that date or information that becomes known to the seller after that date. The disclosures herein shall not be deemed warranties of any kind by the seller or any person representing any party in this transaction.

In this form, "am aware" means to have actual notice or actual knowledge without any specific investigation or inquiry. In this form a "material defect" means a condition that would have a substantial adverse effect on the value of the residential real property or that would significantly impair the health or safety of future occupants of the residential real property unless the seller reasonably believes that the condition has been corrected.

The seller discloses the following information with the knowledge that even though the statements herein are not deemed to be warranties, prospective buyers may choose to rely on this information in deciding whether or not and on what terms to purchase the residential real property.

The seller represents that to the best of his or her actual knowledge, the following statements have been accurately noted as "yes" (correct), "no" (incorrect) or "not applicable" to the property being sold. If the seller indicates that the response to any statement, except number 1, is yes or not applicable, the seller shall provide an explanation, in the additional information area of this form.

YES   NO   N/A

1. ____ ____ ____ Seller has occupied the property within the last 12 months. (No explanation is needed.)
2. ____ ____ ____ I am aware of flooding or recurring leakage problems in the crawlspace or basement.
3. ____ ____ ____ I am aware that the property is located in a flood plain or that I currently have flood hazard insurance on the property.
4. ____ ____ ____ I am aware of material defects in the basement or foundation (including cracks and bulges).
5. ____ ____ ____ I am aware of leaks or material defects in the roof, ceilings or chimney.
6. ____ ____ ____ I am aware of material defects in the walls or floors.
7. ____ ____ ____ I am aware of material defects in the electrical system.
8. ____ ____ ____ I am aware of material defects in the plumbing system (includes such things as water heater, sump pump, water treatment system, sprinkler system, and swimming pool).
9. ____ ____ ____ I am aware of material defects in the well or well equipment.
10. ____ ____ ____ I am aware of unsafe conditions in the drinking water.
11. ____ ____ ____ I am aware of material defects in the heating, air conditioning, or ventilating systems.
12. ____ ____ ____ I am aware of material defects in the fireplace or woodburning stove.
13. ____ ____ ____ I am aware of material defects in the septic, sanitary sewer, or other disposal system.
14. ____ ____ ____ I am aware of unsafe concentrations of radon on the premises.
15. ____ ____ ____ I am aware of unsafe concentrations of or unsafe conditions relating to asbestos on the premises.
16. ____ ____ ____ I am aware of unsafe concentrations of or unsafe conditions relating to lead paint, lead water pipes, lead plumbing pipes or lead in the soil on the premises.
17. ____ ____ ____ I am aware of mine subsidence, underground pits, settlement, sliding, upheaval, or other earth stability defects on the premises.
18. ____ ____ ____ I am aware of current infestations of termites or other wood boring insects.
19. ____ ____ ____ I am aware of a structural defect caused by previous infestations of termites or other wood boring insects.
20. ____ ____ ____ I am aware of underground fuel storage tanks on the property.
21. ____ ____ ____ I am aware of boundary or lot line disputes.
22. ____ ____ ____ I have received notice of violation of local, state or federal laws or regulations relating to this property, which violation has not been corrected.
23. ____ ____ ____ I am aware that this property has been used for the manufacture of methamphetamine as defined in Section 10 of the Methamphetamine Control and Community Protection Act.

Note: These disclosures are not intended to cover the common elements of a condominium, but only the actual residential real property including limited common elements allocated to the exclusive use thereof that form an integral part of the condominium unit.

Note: These disclosures are intended to reflect the current condition of the premises and do not include previous problems, if any, that the seller reasonably believes have been corrected.

If any of the above are marked "not applicable" or "yes", please explain here or use additional pages, if necessary:

_____
_____
_____

Check here if additional pages used: ____

Seller certifies that seller has prepared this statement and certifies that the information provided is based on the actual notice or actual knowledge of the seller without any specific investigation or inquiry on the part of the seller. The seller hereby authorizes any person representing any principal in this transaction to provide a copy of this report, and to disclose any information in the report, to any person in connection with any actual or anticipated sale of the property.

Seller: _____ Date: _____
Seller: _____ Date: _____

PROSPECTIVE BUYER IS AWARE THAT THE PARTIES MAY CHOOSE TO NEGOTIATE AN AGREEMENT FOR THE SALE OF THE PROPERTY SUBJECT TO ANY OR ALL MATERIAL DEFECTS DISCLOSED IN THIS REPORT ("AS IS"). THIS DISCLOSURE IS NOT A SUBSTITUTE FOR ANY INSPECTIONS OR WARRANTIES THAT THE PROSPECTIVE BUYER OR SELLER MAY WISH TO OBTAIN OR NEGOTIATE. THE FACT THAT THE SELLER IS NOT AWARE OF A PARTICULAR CONDITION OR PROBLEM IS NO GUARANTEE THAT IT DOES NOT EXIST. PROSPECTIVE BUYER IS AWARE THAT HE MAY REQUEST AN INSPECTION OF THE PREMISES PERFORMED BY A QUALIFIED PROFESSIONAL.

Prospective Buyer: _____ Date: _____ Time: _____
Prospective Buyer: _____ Date: _____ Time: _____

108 Revised 08/09   COPYRIGHT © BY ILLINOIS ASSOCIATION OF REALTORS®

Get Your Bonuses at
http://www.SellingHousesExposed.com/bonus

ILLINOIS ASSOCIATION OF REALTORS®
MOLD DISCLOSURE

Printed Name(s) of Seller(s) _____

Printed Name(s) of Buyer(s) _____

Property Address _____

1.   **SELLER DISCLOSURE.** To the best of Seller's actual knowledge, Seller represents:

   a.   The property described herein ❑ **has** ❑ **has not** been previously tested for molds, fungi, mildew and similar organisms ("molds");

Note: If answer to a. is "has not," then skip b. and c. and go to Section #2.
   If answer to a. is "has," then complete b. and c.

   b.   The molds found ❑ **were** ❑ **were not** identified as toxic or harmful molds;

   c.   With regard to any molds that were found, measures ❑ **were** ❑ **were not** taken to remove those molds.

Buyers Initials

❑   ❑   2. **MOLD INSPECTIONS.** Molds, fungi, mildew, and similar organisms may exist in the property of which the Seller is unaware and has no actual knowledge. These contaminant's generally grow in places where there is excessive moisture, such as where leakage may have occurred in roofs, pipes, walls, plan pots, or where there has been flooding. A professional home inspection may not disclose molds. Buyer may wish to obtain an inspection specifically for molds to more fully determine the condition of the Property and its environmental status. Neither Seller's agents nor Buyer's agents are experts in the field of mold. The Buyers are strongly encouraged to satisfy themselves as to the Property condition.

3.   **RECEIPT OF COPY.** Seller and Buyer has read this Mold Disclosure and by their signatures hereon acknowledge receipt of a copy thereof.

Seller: _____ Date: _____

Seller: _____ Date: _____

Buyer: _____ Date: _____

Buyer: _____ Date: _____

Form 348 9/2003   Copyright© Illinois Association of REALTORS®

Get Your Bonuses at
http://www.SellingHousesExposed.com/bonus

Illinois Association of REALTORS®

DISCLOSURE OF INFORMATION ON RADON HAZARDS
(For Residential Real Property Sales or Purchases)

Radon Warning Statement

Every buyer of any interest in residential real property is notified that the property may present exposure to dangerous levels of indoor radon gas that may place the occupants at risk of developing radon-induced lung cancer. Radon, a Class-A human carcinogen, is the leading cause of lung cancer in non-smokers and the second leading cause overall. The seller of any interest in residential real property is required to provide the buyer with any information on radon test results of the dwelling showing elevated levels of radon in the seller's possession.

The Illinois Emergency Management Agency (IEMA) strongly recommends ALL homebuyers have an indoor radon test performed prior to purchase or taking occupancy, and mitigated if elevated levels are found. Elevated radon concentrations can easily be reduced by a qualified, licensed radon mitigator.

Seller's Disclosure (initial each of the following which applies)

_____(a) Elevated radon concentrations (above EPA or IEMA recommended Radon Action Level) are known to be present within the dwelling. (Explain)

_____(b) Seller has provided the purchaser with all available records and reports pertaining to elevated radon concentrations within the dwelling.

_____(c) Seller either has no knowledge of elevated radon concentrations in the dwelling or prior elevated radon concentrations have been mitigated or remediated.

_____(d) Seller has no records or reports pertaining to elevated radon concentrations within the dwelling.

Purchaser's Acknowledgment (initial each of the following which applies)

_____(e) Purchaser has received copies of all information listed above.

_____(f) Purchaser has received the IEMA approved Radon Disclosure Pamphlet.

Agent's Acknowledgement (initial IF APPLICABLE)

_____(g) Agent has informed the seller of the seller's obligations under Illinois law.

Certification of Accuracy

The following parties have reviewed the information above and each party certifies, to the best of his or her knowledge, that the information he or she has provided is true and accurate.

Seller _____	Date _____
Seller _____	Date _____
Purchaser _____	Date _____
Purchaser _____	Date _____
Agent _____	Date _____
Agent _____	Date _____
Property Address _____	City, State, Zip Code _____

FORM 422 Revised 08-09   COPYRIGHT ILLINOIS ASSOCIATION OF REALTORS

Get Your Bonuses at
http://www.SellingHousesExposed.com/bonus

ILLINOIS ASSOCIATION OF REALTORS

DISCLOSURE OF INFORMATION AND ACKNOWLEDGMENT
LEAD-BASED PAINT AND/OR LEAD BASED PAINT HAZARDS

Lead Warning Statement

Every purchaser of any interest in residential real property on which a residential dwelling was built prior to 1978 is notified that such property may present exposure to lead from lead-based paint that may place young children at risk of developing lead poisoning. Lead poisoning in young children may produce permanent neurological damage, including learning disabilities, reduced intelligence quotient, behavioral problems, and impaired memory. Lead poisoning also poses a particular risk to pregnant women. The seller of any interest in residential real property is required to provide the buyer with any information on lead-based paint hazards from risk assessments or inspections in the seller's possession and notify the buyer of any known lead-based paint hazards. A risk assessment or inspection for possible lead-based paint hazards is recommended prior to purchase.

PropertyAddress _____

Seller's Disclosure (initial)

_____(a)   Presence of lead-based paint and/or lead-based paint hazards (check one below):

      ☐   Known lead-based paint and/or lead-based paint hazards are present in the housing (explain):

      _____

      _____

      ☐   Seller has no knowledge of lead-based paint and/or lead-based paint hazards in the housing.

_____(b)   Records and Reports available to the seller (check one below):

      ☐   Seller has provided the purchaser with all available records and reports pertaining to lead-based paint and/or lead-based paint hazards in the housing (list documents below):

      _____

      _____

      ☐   Seller has no reports or records pertaining to lead-based paint and/or lead-based paint hazards in the housing.

Purchaser's Acknowledgment (initial)

_____(c)   Purchaser has received copies of all information listed above.

_____(d)   Purchaser has received the pamphlet *Protect Your Family From Lead in Your Home.*

_____(e)   Purchaser has (check one below):

      ☐   Received a 10-day opportunity (or mutually agreed upon period) to conduct a risk assessment or inspection of the presence of lead-based paint or lead-based paint hazards; or

      ☐   Waived the opportunity to conduct a risk assessment or inspection for the presence of lead-based paint and/or lead-based paint hazards.

Agent's Acknowledgment (initial)

_____(f)   Agent has informed the seller of the seller's obligations under 42 U.S.C. 4852d and is aware of his/her responsibility to ensure compliance.

Certification of Accuracy

The following parties have reviewed the information above and certify to the best of their knowledge, that the information they have provided is true and accurate.

Seller _____   Date / /   Purchaser _____   Date / /

Seller _____   Date / /   Purchaser_____   Date / /

Agent _____   Date / /   Agent _____   Date / /

Form 420   Revised 8/2004   *(This disclosure form should be attached to the Contract to Purchase)*

Get Your Bonuses at
http://www.SellingHousesExposed.com/bonus

A Free Gift for You!

As a thank you for reading my book I want to give you several additional bonuses worth $477!

Visit http://www.SellingHousesExposed.com/bonus to download them all!

ABOUT THE AUTHOR

Brian T. Wolf is a residential real estate expert with more than 10 years' experience as an investor, owner, and broker. Brian honed his Midwestern work ethic serving 6 years in the Illinois Air National Guard while completing his bachelor's degree at the University of Illinois at Urbana-Champaign. In addition to spending time with his wife and two children, Brian is active in the Arlington Heights Chamber of Commerce, serving as Membership Chair for his CHAMPPS group, and has earned the Competent Communicator designation as a member of the Arlington Heights Toastmasters Club.

www.ingramcontent.com/pod-product-compliance
Lightning Source LLC
Chambersburg PA
CBHW051338170526
45166CB00002B/866